Studies in applied regional science

This series in applied regional, urban and
environmental analysis aims to provide
regional scientists with a set of adequate tools
for empirical regional analysis and for practical regional planning problems. The major
emphasis in this series will be upon the
applicability of theories and methods in the
field of regional science; these will be presented in a form which can be readily used
by practitioners. Both new applications of
existing knowledge and newly developed ideas
will be published in the series.

Studies in applied regional science Vol. 13

Editor-in-Chief

P. Nijkamp
Free University, Amsterdam

Editorial Board

Å.E Andersson
University of Gothenburg, Gothenburg
W. Isard
Regional Science Institute, Philadelphia
L.H. Klaassen
Netherlands Economic Institute, Rotterdam
I. Masser
State University, Utrecht
N. Sakashita
Osaka University, Osaka

Urban residential location models

Stephen H. Putman
Associate Professor of City and Regional Planning,
University of Pennsylvania

Martinus Nijhoff Publishing
Boston/The Hague/London

Library of Congress Cataloging in Publication Data

Main entry under title:

Urban residential location models.

    (Studies in applied regional science ; v. 13)
      1. Land use, Urban--Mathematical models.
  2. Cities and towns--Growth--Mathematical models.
  3. Residential mobility--Mathematical models.
I. Putman, Stephen H. II. Series.
HD111.U72   333.7'7   78-12285
ISBN 0-89838-011-1
ISBN 90 207 0785 X

Distributors outside of North America:
Kluwer Academic Publishers Group
Distribution Centre
P.O. Box 322
3300 AH Dordrecht, The Netherlands

Photoset in Malta by Interprint (Malta) Ltd.

Printed and bound in the United States of America

Preface

The decade of the 1970's has seen substantial improvement in our understanding of the determinants of urban spatial patterns. It is typical of western science and technology of the past several centuries that these advances in urban spatial analysis have resulted from the efforts of many individuals. No one of these claims to have found *the* answer; rather, each contributes some additional understanding of a rather complex set of interrelated phenomena. All of this most recent work, in one way or another, rests on preliminary analysis work done in the previous ten to fifteen years. Those earlier efforts are the subject of this book.

A very few studies of urban spatial patterns were done prior to 1960. However, it was not until then, with the coming of age of electronic data processing machinery, that work began in earnest. Many theories and theoretical models of urban form were postulated, and some were tested. Often the tests were inconclusive or unsuccessful. The theories often lacked consistency and coherence. Some of the testing was inadequate or even inappropriate. Much of the research was done amidst the turmoil (and sometimes chaos) of attempted (and often premature) application. The results were frequently incompletely described, if described at all. Yet, out of all this, there began to emerge some clearer notion of the determinants of urban spatial patterns.

The purpose of this book is to collect, excerpt, and comment on, the most important of these earlier attempts at urban spatial modelling. Many of the studies described here failed to meet their stated objectives. However, both the failures and successes contributed to progress in the field. Anyone who is actually, or likely to be, involved with urban spatial analysis can profit from a knowledge of the successes and failures reported here. The intent of this book is not to present the current state-of-the-art, but rather to describe the antecedents, both theoretical and empirical, of the current work in the field.

Finally, it is clear that it would not have been possible to include here all the material which was potentially includable. The selection made was an attempt to best describe the evolution of theory and application of urban residential models. Some other work, equal in quality, was not included in order to avoid repetition of key ideas. I hope that unincluded authors will not take too great an offense, where none was intended. To those who have permitted their work to be included here, I extend my thanks.

Stephen H. Putman
Philadelphia, Pennsylvania
March 1978

Contents

1. Introduction

1.1. INTRODUCTION

During the past twenty years there have been many attempts made to develop computer simulations of urban systems. These attempts have ranged from quite modest to almost absurdly grand. Some have been rather successful while others were abysmal failures. To date, the efforts which have to some extent failed outnumber those which have succeeded. Yet all-in-all there has been substantial progress made, from a situation of great optimism and little knowledge to a more conservative position of guarded optimism with much more knowledge of urban phenomena. The purpose of this book is to review, with the advantage of hindsight, the progress which has been made. The intent of such a review is not only to record that which has been accomplished, but to also recall that which has failed. It is our hope that the information thus presented will help guide and enlighten future research efforts in the field.

The literature in this field has become quite voluminous, with the author's private collection of reports, papers, reprints, etc. filling the better part of half a dozen file drawers. Consequently selecting excerpts, along with preparing interpretive and classificatory prose in such a way that the important material is presented in a reasonably compact form was no small task. It would have been much less difficult to prepare seven or eight volumes such as this than it was to prepare this one volume plus its contemplated mate.

The first cut through the material eliminated all work lacking a spatially disaggregated orientation. The second cut eliminated work whose principal focus was on representation and simulation of transportation networks and the flows on them. This left a still considerable amount of work whose primary concern was with the spatial distribution of economic and demographic activities in urban areas. This material was then divided into residence location, employment location, and 'other'. Well over half of this, perhaps as much as two thirds, was focussed on questions regarding residence location. Accordingly, this volume is devoted exclusively to research and application efforts concerning residence location. When, as is sometimes the case, a particular research effort included analyses of both residence and employment, the emphasis here, both in excerpts and prose, is on the residence component of the work. The planned companion volume will take up the employment analyses along with miscellaneous 'other' efforts. All the material in both volumes is strictly urban-metropolitan in focus.

1.2. A HISTORICAL NOTE

Many of the early urban simulation projects were organized around the interdisciplinary approach which derived from the operations research and systems analysis approaches of the post World War II decade. Often the most vocal of these early proponents of urban modelling were riding the euphoric crest of the wave of apparent successes of operations research and systems analysis of the 1950's. After the successful analysis and project scheduling of the U.S. Navy's Polaris missile project, and successful simulation of the spares inventory for the entire U.S. Air Force, the simulation of household location in the metropolis seemed to be a perfectly reasonable undertaking. It was assumed that the apparent regularities in urban form could easily be replicated with the computer simulation techniques then available. There was much discussion as to the relative merits of various computer simulation languages such as SIMSCRIPT, GASP, etc. and rather less discussion as to the precise theoretical underpinnings of such models. With the passing of almost two full decades the rash naïveté of this attitude has become painfully obvious.

The self-confidence of these early modellers, the lack of any visible alternative's holding any hope of comprehensive, systematic analysis of the emerging urban problems, and, indeed, the temper of the times all combined to yield substantial public funds for urban simulation projects. There were, however, two major factors which virtually guaranteed the failure of these efforts. The first factor was the utter lack of understanding of the complex relationships which determine urban form and the associated lack of any real body of knowledge on which to base the work. The second factor was that the funding, performance, and scheduling of these efforts treated them not as basic research and development projects, but as a part of ongoing policy analysis and other planning agency activities. Looking back on the situation, it is clear now that many of these projects were predestined to fail. It was as if Roosevelt, on hearing of the feasibility of constructing atomic bombs and thus ending the war, had loaded a few physicists and their equipment into a large airplane bound for the battlefront with orders to build the bombs on the way.

As if the above factors were not sufficient, there were further problems occasioned by the fact that many of these modelling projects were conducted by private consulting firms. Thus the success, or at least the perceived success of these projects had 'life-or-death' consequences for some of the organizations doing them. This factor alone is undoubtably one of the largest single reasons for the unutterably poor documentation of the models and their actual successes or failures.

In view of all this it cannot be considered surprising that by the mid-1960's a strong anti-urban-modelling sentiment began to appear amongst planners and policy makers. This sentiment has been reported and repeated by some of the planning professionals who were entering the field at that time. As is always the case, different people learned different things from this experience. What was learned depended very much on what the learner desired to learn.

In the field of astronomy the collection and tabulation of data on planetary motion began during the time of the early Greeks. The first systematic explanation of their movements (Ptolemy of Alexandria, circa A.D. 150) resulted from five centuries of discussion. This system, using only components of circular motion, remained the accepted description for nearly fifteen centuries until the revisions of Copernicus (circa 1500), who retained the notion of circular motion, but put the sun in the center of the system. Shortly thereafter, based on five year's work with an inherited data set accumulated over many years of observation, Kepler revised the system description to one of elliptical orbits with the sun at one focus of the ellipse. Three hundred more years of refinement of tools, theories, and data sets were to elapse before the discovery of the seventh planet (the first planet to be discovered in more than two thousand years). Only sixty years, filled with revisions and extensions to planetary theory, improvement in observational techniques, and researches through early data sets, were to elapse before the discovery of the eighth planet. This discovery was based on a prediction from a set of equations.

This astronomical analogy is obvious. Even though we are used, in this last quarter of the twentieth century, to rapid technological advance, twenty years is not over long for our understanding of the complexities of urban systems to have reached their current state; nor is it reasonable to expect them to have reached perfection after such a time span.

1.3. THE PREMISE

The premise of this book is that advances in the understanding of urban spatial phenomena, as in many other fields, come through an iterative process of theoretical development, empirical testing, theory revision, empirical testing, etc. Or, as Leontief has postulated for economics:

> True advance can be achieved only through an iterative process in which improved theoretical formulation raises new empirical questions and the answers to these questions, in their turn, lead to new theoretical insights. The 'givens' of today become the 'unknowns' that will have to be explained tomorrow.[1]

Special issues of the *Journal of the American Institute of Planners* were published in May 1959 and May 1965 to publicize the modelling work then being contemplated or completed. Models were widely discussed, criticized, and sometimes revised. The backlash of the late 1960's along with generally accurate but myopic reviews such as those by Lee[2] and Brewer[3] brought most large model projects to a stop for several years. This was, nevertheless, a productive time. Work continued, with substantial theoretical advances, in Great Britain. This new work is well described in recent books by Wilson[4] and Batty.[5]

The material in this book represents the salient theoretical and empirical works leading up to this newer work, but does not attempt to describe the newer work itself. Rather, it provides the basis upon which and the context within which this new work has developed. Further, by documenting much of what has gone before, it will provide useful insights as to directions which might yet yield further useful results, while avoiding unnecessary repetition of previously unsuccessful efforts.

1. Leontief, W., 'Theoretical Assumptions and Nonobserved Facts', *American Economic Review*, vol. 61, no. 1, pp. 1–7, 1971.
2. Lee, D. B., 'Requiem for Large Scale Models', Journal of the *American Institute of Planners*, vol. 39, no. 3, pp. 163–178, 1973.
3. Brewer, G., *Politicians, Bureaucrats, and the Consultant*, Basic Books, New York, 1973.
4. Wilson, A., *Urban and Regional Models in Geography and Planning*, Wiley, London, 1974.
5. Batty, M., *Urban Modelling*, Cambridge University Press, London, 1976.

1.4. CLASSIFYING RESIDENCE LOCATION MODELS

The development of classification procedures is a preliminary and often necessary first step in the study of objects or phenomena. In such sciences as biology, periodic revisions of classifications have been undertaken as knowledge about the organisms being classified has increased or as new organisms have been discovered. Often, the defining of criteria for inclusion or exclusion of a particular organism in or from a group forces the recognition and/or resolution of important conceptual questions. Similarly, the organizing of items into systematic arrays has sometimes exposed gaps to be filled by subsequent research (e.g. the periodic table of elements).

The fact that this volume is devoted only to residential models reflects several classification decisions already mentioned. Further, it is to be noted that a special effort has been made here to separate the residential location sections out of the models discussed in order to describe them. This is done so that to the extent possible, the discussion may be freed from any overall system in which the residential model may have been embedded. On the other hand, where operational results are described they are often the results of model systems which include constraint procedures as well. Hopefully, this results in a more lucid presentation of the actual processes by which various models accomplish their estimating tasks.

At the center of every residence location model there is a function or set of functions (equations) which performs the actual spatial location or allocation procedure. These functions are the explicit statement of the procedure by which the particular model attempts to replicate and/or describe residence location. It is by the nature of these functions that the models may be classified. It is interesting to note that the names assigned to these different classes have changed over time as our knowledge about the models and the urban systems they try to simulate has changed. Also, different authors, often from other disciplines, have assigned the same model to different classifications. The scheme proposed here tries to take some of these factors into account.

The class of models formerly called 'behavioral models', and containing the Lowry model as its most widely known representative, might be better called 'macro-behavioral' or 'macro-descriptive'. A useful way of thinking about this class of models is that they attempt to describe behavior at a level of detail similar to what would be observed from an airplane two to three miles above the city.

Another group of models formerly included under the 'behavioral' classification might better be termed 'micro-descriptive'. This group includes models such as the Herbert-Stevens model, and the work done at the University of North Carolina at Chapel Hill. These models attempt to describe the decision-making processes of individual households and/or housing developers. These are considered by some economists to be the only models which can be properly termed 'behavioral'. Recent theoretical research has, however, demonstrated that at least some of their constructs (e.g. those based on transport cost minimization or on household utility maximization) can be shown to be special cases of the largest group of macro-descriptive models. This movement towards a unification of theory is most encouraging and augers well for the future of urban spatial models generally.

The complement to the above classes is, of course, the 'non-behavioral models'. These might better be termed 'associative' than 'non-behavioral'. The structure of this type model tends to consist of one or more multi-variate linear equations. While various hypotheses as to the determinants of urban form are used to determine which variables are used in these equations, the equations themselves presuppose no particular functional form (except linear multivariate) for the model. The precise determination of the form of the model is therefore left to be determined by the regression analyses used to calculate the equation parameters. The best known example of this type model is the widely used EMPIRIC.

This general classification scheme is employed to organize the material which follows. Chapter 2 contains material about associative models, principally EMPIRIC. Chapter 3 contains material about macro-behavioral models, in this case almost exclusively Lowry and Lowry derivative models. Chapter 4 is something of a potpourri, containing some material on non-Lowry macro-behavioral models and some material on micro-behavioral models. The last chapter, as is customary, attempts to tie the work together as well as to point towards desirable future work.

2. Empiric model applications

This portion of the book is almost exclusively devoted to a single model and its applications. In U.S. planning practice the EMPIRIC model, beginning with work done by the Traffic Research Corporation for the Boston Regional Planning Project in 1963 and continuing through the early 1970's, has been the single most widely applied urban land use model. Its success, despite the barrage of criticism which has been leveled at it (as described in the following pages) is due in no small measure to its robustness in terms of its fit to base year data, and to the concerted development and sales efforts of its progenitors and their successors (T.R.C. and Peat Marwick Mitchell respectively).

At the outset of T.R.C.'s Boston project two alternative model constructs were developed and tested, EMPIRIC and POLIMETRIC. The EMPIRIC model was developed in the form of simultaneous linear difference equations, while POLIMETRIC was in the form of simultaneous non-linear differential equations. In both models the dependent variables were changes in regional share of a particular locating activity in each particular zone. Both models achieved relatively good fits to base year data for the Boston metropolitan region. POLIMETRIC was very much more demanding of computer time. After comparing the results from the models, development of POLIMETRIC was abandoned in favor of continued work with EMPIRIC.

The excerpt from Hill, Brand, and Hansen describes the initial concepts which resulted in the development of EMPIRIC. The excerpt from the Traffic Research Corporation Final Report describes the formulation of EMPIRIC as implemented.

The results of various EMPIRIC applications have been published in reports from the various agencies sponsoring the work. Six of these applications were summarized and compared as part of a study completed by this author in 1975. The results of this comparison are included in the following pages.

The EMPIRIC model results have spawned few further efforts, in contradistinction to the vast array of Lowry model derivative efforts. The work of Masser, et al. was an attempt to develop an EMPIRIC model for an application in England. While the effort was moderately successful, it has not been followed up. Similarly, Seidman's development of RESLOC as a component of the Penn Jersey Transportation Study's Activities Allocation Model (AAM) was more or less successful but there has not been any further work done with it either.

When, in the early 1960's, the first urban computer simulation models were being developed, one of the principal goals was to develop the capability of assessing the consequences of various urban renewal plans on the spatial distribution of activities. It was hoped that different public policies capable of altering the mix of activities in a zone could enter the models in various forms. The arrival or departure of an employment facility would induce significant effects in the model outputs. The arrival of a number of households of a particular income class might well result in changes in location of other households and perhaps of some employees too. Similarly the departure of a group of households would probably further induce changes in a zone's activity mix.

Further, it was hoped that the density and degree, or extent, of development in a zone would also be affected by policy inputs. Clearance of certain types of structure would change density as would the erection of new structures. The construction of large new developments, say of single family residential homes, or – at a different density – of apartments, would change both the zone's density as well as its extent of development. These changes would induce other changes, both in employment and in population location. In a related way, changes in the amount of land available in a zone should affect future location of activities in a zone. More stringent land use controls, having the effect of reducing available land, will change the pattern of activities locating in a zone. Similarly holding back land from development should also result in changed location patterns.

Finally, the spatial separation of activities from each other was expected to be a key variable in these models. This variable is usually expressed in terms of travel times and/or travel costs between zones and activities. Thus any substantial change in the transportation facilities should result in a change in activity distributions.

Many modelling projects were begun, with very few being successfully completed. It was a chaotic time for urban modelling. Each model had its proponents who claimed that their's was 'the way'. Not many of these models have survived, though there continue to be occasional uses of one-time only models or newly developed ones. The majority of recent model applications have been of either EMPIRIC or Lowry derivative models, with basic research efforts being performed independent of ongoing applications.

Despite the popularity of the EMPIRIC model, it has several crucial short-comings, particularly in the context of the above mentioned aspirations of most modelling efforts. In 1964 Franklin M. Fisher and Louis Lefeber prepared a review of the early EMPIRIC work.[1] One of the first points made is that urban spatial distributions are quite stable. This implies that one may obtain a good estimate of an urban spatial distribution at time $t + 1$ by simply assuming that it will be very much the same as it was at time t, with perhaps some modest trend adjustments.[2] The fact is that many of the more complex urban simulation models do not achieve fits to base year data which are as good as simple trend estimates, at least in the case of short term (5–10 year) forecasts. If, however, the forecasting procedure is in-tended to provide policy responsive outputs, then trend estimates are useless. It is the possibility that they would be policy responsive that has been used to justify virtually all urban simulation model undertakings. Thus Fisher and Lefeber say:

To summarize: if a model is to be used for policy prediction or even if it is considered desirable to forecast the effects of changes in the pattern of events outside the ... area, the model must be of a structural nature. It must lay bare so far as possible the causal relationships among the variables and the causal effects of policy. This is far more important (and far more difficult) than the perfecting of simple forecasts for periods in which little of interest happens to destroy historical continuity.

The building of such a structural model requires an artful blend of economic and socio-logical theory with statistical and econometric technique. The results must be judged both by the reasonableness of the causal patterns estimated and by the conformance of the model to empirical data. In addition, both the theoretical basis of the model and the statistical techniques used to estimate the values of its parameters must be logically con-sistent, each in itself, and each with the other. While conformity with the facts must always be of paramount consideration, models cannot be compared on the basis of goodness of fit alone. The models which yield the best fit to historical data are also likely to be those which

1. This rather elusive document was titled 'Review and Evaluation of the Work Undertaken by Traffic Research Corporation for the Boston Regional Planning Project', and ap-parently received very limited circulation. It contains a scathing review of the TRC work which, while quite gratuitous in some ways, contains some very telling comments re-garding urban model work in general.
2. This is also true for much larger regions as well and is discussed in the author's mono-graph *An Empirical Model of Regional Growth*, Monograph Series Number Six, Regional Science Research Institute, Philadelphia, Pa. pp. 33–39, 179–180, 1975.

yield the least structural information. Unless a good fit is backed up by a quantitative causal analysis, it is unlikely to be preserved in interesting future circumstances. Unless a model yields causal information it is likely to be useless for planning purposes, if more is desired than a simple forecast.

After some further discussion of reduced form equation models vs. structural equation models they conclude, correctly, that EMPIRIC is a reduced form model. From this follows the most telling criticism of all of the models discussed in this chapter.

Third, and perhaps most important, one often has rather definite ideas as to the signs and general magnitudes of the parameters of the *structural* equations. (For example, demand curves are generally supposed to have negative slopes.) By obtaining structural estimates, one can test the model by seeing whether the parameter estimates obtained are consistent with those ideas. Since several different models are likely to fit the data equally well, the choice between them may crucially depend on the way in which the structural parameters stand up to this sort of test. No such test can generally be performed on the parameters of the reduced form which are complicated functions of the structural parameters.... One cannot have a model in which every variable depends on every other one and also have a model whose structural parameters can be consistently estimated. One must specify in advance, from information outside the data, that certain variables do not appear in certain equations. If such variables really do not appear, then it may be possible to know this. If this is not known in advance, or if it is in fact false, then no amount of data handling can result in consistent estimates even if it apparently sets the appropriate number of coefficients equal to zero. The requirement is a logical and factual one, not a mere mathematical nicety.

One reason for the popularity of EMPIRIC is that it achieves good fits to base data. Unfortunately it is not adequately sensitive to changes in input variables. This is probably due to its lack of an explicit theoretical form and confirms the arguments of Fisher and Lefeber. The model has, however, been very useful for shorter term urban projections and it should be remembered that at first, even its authors claimed associative validity, rather than any genuine theoretical validity.[3] Until recently the best of the Lowry derivative models in current U.S. use would not have compared especially well to EMPIRIC. Their theoretical structure is rudimentary, their disaggregation of population types is accomplished independent of the location procedure, and they rely on several exogenously defined constraint mechanisms to achieve good fits to base year data. Further, there was no standardized procedure for preparing a statistically valid estimation of these early Lowry type models' parameters. It is no wonder then that EMPIRIC was a rather popular alternative. It was only the further research

3. Hill, D. M., D. Brand, and W. B. Hansen, 'Prototype Development of Statistical Land-Use Prediction Model for Greater Boston Region' *Highway Research Record* no. 114, pp. 51–70, 1966.

suggested by the Lowry construct that led to models which now surpass EMPIRIC in most respects. For the time, despite these objections, EMPIRIC was a beginning, and served its purpose well.

2.2. PROTOTYPE DEVELOPMENT OF STATISTICAL LAND-USE PREDICTION MODEL FOR GREATER BOSTON REGION

Donald M. Hill, D. Brand, and W. B. Hansen

Highway Research Record No. 114 (1966) pp. 51–70

The underlying concept of the EMPIRIC model is that the development patterns of urban activities are interrelated in a systematic manner which provides a reasonable basis for their prediction. The model provides the formal mathematical mechanism for evaluating the extent of these interrelations between activities. The only restriction imposed by the model is that the interrelationships be expressed so that the influences of variables are additive. Accordingly, the model assumes a linear form. Any desired combination or transformation of variables may be introduced to describe the urban activities whose locational pattern we wish to measure and predict. The model requires exogenous specification (i.e. external predictions) of regional growth totals for all urban activities to be projected.

To describe the model, it is convenient to define a number of quantities as follows:

1. The region is divided into a number of small areas called *subregions*.
2. The purpose of the model is to predict the amounts of several urban activities in each subregion at the end of a given forecast period. These activities are called *located variables*, signifying that the task of the model is to allocate given regional totals of these variables at the end of the forecast period to the subregions comprising the region.
3. It has been found that the locations and intensities of several urban activities are related to development patterns of one or more variables in a casual manner, that is, whose presence or absence in a subregion, or whose ease of accessibility to the subregion, may be said to influence the amounts of one or more located variables in each subregion. These influencing variables are called *locator variables*.

The model is formulated to explain changes in activity levels of urban subregions over one or more time periods. Accordingly, the concept of the model may be stated as follows: the change in the subregional share of a located variable in each subregion is proportional to the change in the subregional share of all other located variables in the subregion, the change in the subregional share of a number of locator variables in the subregion, and the value of the subregional shares of other locator variables.

The concept of the model may be stated by:

$$
\frac{R_{il}^{(t+1)}}{\sum\limits_{l=1}^{L} R_{il}^{(t+1)}} - \frac{R_{il}^{(t)}}{\sum\limits_{l=1}^{L} R_{il}} = \sum\limits_{\substack{j=1 \\ j \neq i}}^{N} a_{ij} \left[\frac{R_{jl}^{(t+1)}}{\sum\limits_{l=1}^{L} R_{jl}^{(t+1)}} - \frac{R_{jl}^{(t)}}{\sum\limits_{l=1}^{L} R_{jl}^{(t)}} \right] +
$$

$$
\sum\limits_{k=1}^{M-m} b_{ik} \left[\frac{Z_{jl}^{(t+1)}}{\sum\limits_{l=1}^{L} Z_{kl}^{(t+1)}} - \frac{Z_{kl}^{(t)}}{\sum\limits_{l=1}^{L} Z_{kl}^{(t)}} \right] +
$$

$$
\sum\limits_{k=M-m+1}^{M} b_{ik} \left[\frac{1}{L} - \frac{Z_{kl}^{(t)}}{\sum\limits_{l=1}^{L} Z_{kl}^{(t)}} \right]
$$

where

$R_{i,l}$	= level of located variable i in subregion;
Z_{kl}	= level of locator variable k in subregion;
L	= number of subregions, $l = 1, 2, \ldots, L$;
N	= number of located variables, $i = 1, \ldots, i, j, \ldots, N$;
M	= number of locator variables, $k = 1, 2, \ldots, M$;
$(t+1), (t)$	= (located and locator) variables at end and beginning of forecast or calibration interval, respectively; and
a_{ij}, b_{ik}	= coefficients expressing interrelationships among variables.

There is one equation for each located variable i. The coefficients a and b are determined by simultaneous regression analysis of the data from two past points in time (i.e. the model is calibrated).

After determining the coefficients, the equations are used to estimate future subregional shares of each located variable by substituting into each equation the pertinent values of the locator variables for that subregion and solving the equations simultaneously for the subregional located variables. To obtain the forecast in absolute rather than relative values, the subregional shares at the end of the forecast interval are multiplied by the exogenous (i.e. externally forecast) control figure for the total of each located variable in the study region.

Development of empiric model

Development of the EMPIRIC model required detailed analyses of cause and effect relationships between development patterns of all land-use categories, as well as detailed analyses of the independence and interdependence of locational groupings of urban activities at the subregional level. An associative or statistical model rather than a true behavioral model was the goal, since it was felt that existing theories of urban development and data sources were not far enough advanced to permit the development of a suitable behavioral type of land-use model.

2.3. FINAL REPORT: DEVELOPMENT AND CALIBRATION OF THE EMPIRIC LAND USE FORECASTING MODEL FOR 626 TRAFFIC ZONES

Traffic Research Corporation

Prepared for the Eastern Massachusetts Regional Planning Project, Feb. 1967

Development of the prototype land use forecasting techniques

To ensure that a land use forecasting technique would be developed which would be satisfactory for producing forecasts for the 626 traffic zones comprising the Eastern Massachusetts Region, Traffic Research Corporation developed to the prototype or experimental stage two separate land use forecasting techniques. These techniques, called POLIMETRIC and EMPIRIC, respectively, were described in a draft procedures manual prepared in late 1963 for the Planning Project. At this stage of development, the capacities of these techniques or models were limited with respect to the numbers of land use categories which could be forecast and with respect to the fineness with which the study area could be subdivided. However, the calibration, prediction, and reliability testing mechanisms of both techniques were programmed for an electronic computer, and both techniques were fully operational.

The underlying concept of both forecasting models is that the development patterns of urban activities are interrelated in a systematic manner which provides a reasonable basis for their prediction. The models provided the formal mathematical mechanisms for evaluating the extent of interrelations between variables; they thereby may be calibrated for use as predictive tools.

Basic concept of the POLIMETRIC model
The POLIMETRIC model is a dynamic model, calibrated using data measuring the levels of and changes in all pertinent activities over one or more time periods, and is formulated in terms of differential equations. The basic overall concept of the model may be stated mathematically by means of the following equation:

$$\frac{dR_{ih}}{dt} = p_i R_{ih} + \sum_{g=1}^{H} M_{igh} - \sum_{g=1}^{H} M_{ihg} \tag{1}$$

where

$h =$ one of the subregions or zones comprising the study region = $1, 2, \ldots, g, \ldots, H$

$i =$ one of the activities to be forecast in each zone = $1, 2, \ldots, j, \ldots, N$

$R_{ih} =$ the value of activity i in zone h

$t =$ time

$P_i =$ the percentage regional growth of activity i during the forecasting interval under consideration

$\sum_{g=1}^{H} M_{igh} =$ the total amount of activity i which migrates from all other zones g to zone h during the forecasting interval

$\sum_{g=1}^{H} M_{ihg} =$ the total amount of activity i which migrates to all other zones g from zone h during the forecasting interval.

Expressed in words, equation (1) states that the change in activity i in zone h is equal to the share of region-wide growth (or decline) in activity i which zone h would receive if all zones achieved equal relative growth (or decline), plus the total in-migration of activity i from all other zones to zone h, minus the total out-migration of activity i from zone h to all other zones. Since the region-wide percentage growth of activity i is externally specified, the key to the realism or non-realism of this equation is the manner in which the in-migration and out-migration terms are defined and calculated. It is postulated that the migration of activity i from zone g to zone h varies directly as the value of activity i in zone g, varies directly as the effective area of the receiving zone h, and varies directly with the difference between the desirabilities of zone h and zone g for activity i. Stated mathematically:

$$M_{igh} = R_{ig}E_h \exp\left[D_{ih} - D_{ig} + M_i\right] \tag{2}$$

where

M_{igh} = the migration of activity i from zone g to zone h during the forecasting interval under consideration

R_{ig} = the value of activity i in donating zone g

E_h = the effective area of receiving zone h

D_{ih} = the desirability of zone h for activity i

D_{ig} = the desirability of zone g for activity i

M_i = the mobility of activity i (discussed further below).

The meaning of the exponential term can be made clearer by observing the graph drawn below, showing migration plotted against the difference in desirabilities.

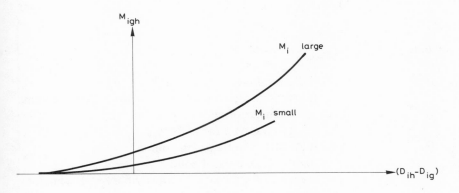

The use of the exponential function gives a reasonable type of migration function, increasing ever more sharply for larger differences between the desirability of zone h and that of zone g. The fact that the migration of activity i from zone g to zone h has a finite positive value even when the desirability of zone g for activity i is greater than the desirability of zone h for activity i, is a means of taking into account random or irrational migration which may go counter to the relative desirabilities of the two zones when both are of almost equal desirability.

The graph also illustrates the role of the mobility term. This term allows the model to simulate the fact that some activities show a greater propensity to move than do others, all other things being equal. A large value of the mobility term for activity i indicates that activity experiences relatively high values of migration even for small or negative differences in zonal desirabilities. A small value for the mobility term indicates an activity which experiences relatively small amounts of migration, even when the receiving zone is considerably more desirable than the donating zone for that activity.

Again, equation (2) merely provides a reasonable framework for describing quantitatively the manner in which interzonal migration depends on relative zonal desirabilities and the mobility of each activity. The degree of realism of this equation is determined by the manner in which these desirabilities and mobilities are defined and calculated.

The desirability of zone h for activity i is defined to be the sum of two terms: the weighted sum of the intensity of all activities in zone h; and the weighted sum of the accessibility to zone h of all other activities in all other zones g. Stated mathematically:

$$D_{ih} = \sum_{j=1}^{N} (a_{ij} R_{jh}/E_h) + \sum_{j=1}^{N} (b_{ij} A_{jh}) \qquad (3)$$

where

$D_{ih} =$ the desirability of zone h for activity i

$a_{ij} =$ the weighting factor which describes by what amount the intensity of activity j in zone h affects the desirability of zone h for activity i

$R_{jh} =$ the value of activity j in zone h

$E_h =$ the effective area of zone h

$b_{ij} =$ the weighting factor which describes by what amount the accessibility to zone h of activity j in all other zones g, affects the desirability of zone h for activity i

$A_{jh} = \sum_{g=1}^{H} (R_{jg} r_{hg}) =$ the accessibility of zone h of activity j in all other zones g

$r_{hg} = \exp^{-\beta t hg} =$ the friction factor representing the manner in which accessibility between zones h and g decreases as the interzonal travel time, t_{hg}, increases

β = the 'beta factor,' or friction factor exponent (empirically derived, and usually set at about 0.05)

t_{hg} = the travel time or time-cost between zone h and zone g.

As was the case for equations (1) and (2), equation (3) is formulated to state as generally as possible the relationship between the dependent variable and the independent variables. In this case, the equation states the manner in which a zone's desirability for one activity varies as the intensity of the activities in the zone itself, as well as the activity levels in all other zones and the amount of travel friction between all other zones and the zone in question. The realism in equation (3), and hence of the entire model, depends on whether it is possible to determine values of a_{ij} and b_{ij} which describe effectively the interrelationships between activities, considered both intrazonally and interzonally.

The coefficients a_{ij}, b_{ij}, and M_i are estimated (i.e. the model is calibrated) by means of special regression techniques developed for this model, carried out on data from two or more time points during the recent past. Each a_{ij} and b_{ij} matrix is dimensioned N by N, where N is the number of activities to be forecast ($i = 1, 2, \ldots, j, \ldots, N$). An additional N mobilities, M_i, (one for each activity i), also have to be determined. Hence, a total of $2N^2 + N$ coefficients must be determined by the regression analysis.

Equation (1) outlines the basic predictive mechanism of the model, where the migrations are defined by equations (2) and (3). There is one such equation (1) describing each activity i in each zone h. Therefore, since there are N activities to be forecast and H zones, the model at full utilization comprises $N \times H$ differential equations of the form of equation (1), whose simultaneous solution for each forecasting interval will provide estimates of the level of each activity in each zone at the end of the interval as well as at optionally specified equally spaced time points during the interval.

Basic concept of the EMPIRIC model

The EMPIRIC model is made up of a system of linear equations for which coefficients of all equations are estimated by simultaneous multiple regression analysis. The model is calibrated by measuring the levels of and changes in all pertinent activities over one or more time periods. The basic overall concept of the model may be stated mathematically by means of the following equation:

$$\sum_{j=1}^{N} a_{ij} R_{jh}(\Delta) + \sum_{k=1}^{N} b_{ik} R_{kh}(t-1) + \sum_{k=N+1}^{M} b_{ik} Z_{kh} = 0 \qquad (4)$$

where

> h = one of the subregions or zones comprising the study region = $1, 2, \ldots, H$
>
> i = one of the (output) activities to be forecast = $1, 2, \ldots, j, \ldots, N$
>
> k = one of the variables whose locations and intensities are related to development patterns of the forecast (output) activities in a causal manner = $1, 2, \ldots, N, \ldots, M$
>
> $R_{jh}(\Delta)$ = the change in the output variable j in zone h from the beginning to the end of a forecast interval
>
> $R_{kh}(t-1)$ = the value of the causal variable k (= output variable j) in zone h at the beginning of a forecast interval
>
> Z_{kh} = the value of the causal variable k in zone h
>
> a_{ij} and b_{ik} = coefficients (a_{ij} = 1 when $i = j$).

This equation thus relates the growth of a single output (dependent) variable i in zone h to: the growth of the other output variables j in zone h; the present amount of the output variable i in zone h; and the amount of the causal variables k in zone h.

The coefficients a_{ij} express the influence of the growths of dependent variables j ($j \neq 1$) on the desirability of zone h for dependent variable i. The coefficients b_{ik} express the influence of independent variables k on the desirability of zone h for dependent variable i. The realism of equation (4) and hence of the entire model depends on whether it is possible to determine values of a_{ij} and b_{ik} which describe effectively the interrelationships between all activities.

The coefficients a_{ij} and b_{ik} are estimated (i.e. the model is calibrated) by means of simultaneous multiple linear regression analysis carried out on data from two time points in the recent past. There are $N \times N$ values of the a_{ij} coefficients and $N \times M$ values of the b_{ik} coefficients to be estimated; or, a total of $N(N + M)$ coefficients. All a_{ij}'s having $i = j$ are set equal to unity, and for proper identification of the equation system, at least $(N - 1)$ of the a_{ij}'s and b_{ik}'s in each equation must be constrained (usually set equal to zero). (The inclusion of all or nearly all of the independent variables in each equation would lead to major problems of coefficient instability, but theoretical analysis shows a sufficient number of the b_{ik}'s to be insignificant in the equations. Consequently, no identification problems are normally encountered.)

Once the model has been calibrated, it is operated in a recursive manner for forecasting purposes. There is one equation for each of the dependent variables in each zone, and the system of equations is solved separately for each zone. At full utilization, therefore, the model comprises N equations per zone of the form outlined above, whose simultaneous solution for a given forecasting interval will provide growths of zonal activity levels during this interval.

2.4. LABORATORY TESTING OF PREDICTIVE LAND USE MODELS: SOME COMPARISONS

S. H. Putman

U.S. Department of Transportation
Office of Transportation Systems Analyses and Information
October 1976

Calibration of EMPIRIC

The EMPIRIC model was first described more than a decade ago, and has since seen application in more than a dozen U.S. cities. Peat, Marwick, Mitchell and Company (hereafter referred to as PMM) have been the principal proponents and practicioners of EMPIRIC. In past years they have generously supplied reports and data from these applications to the Principal Investigator of this study. Consequently there were detailed descriptions of previously estimated EMPIRIC models available for this study. These reports were available for the Atlanta, Boston, Denver, Puget Sound, Twin Cities (Minneapolis-St. Paul), and Washington, D.C. metropolitan areas. In addition there were packages of computer programs and data sets available for Boston, Twin Cities, and Washington. An idea of the sizes of these metropolitan areas as modelled may be obtained by reference to table 2.4.1. Reviewing each of these applications led to the conclusion that while many of the variables used were similar from one application to the next, (the equation structure was, of course, identical), the specific variables used were different in each application. The dependent variables

TABLE 2.4.1.   Comparative sizes of EMPIRIC application regions.

Name of region	Population	Employment	Year	Counties in study region
Atlanta, Ga.	1.0 million	605 thousand	1961	7
	1.4 million	n.a.	1970	
Boston, Mass.	3.4 million	n.a.	1960	n.a.
Denver, Colo.	0.9 million	388 thousand	1960	5
	1.2 million	533 thousand	1970	
Puget Sound, Wash.	1.7 million	610 thousand	1970	4
Twin Cities, Minn.	1.5 million	610 thousand	1960	7
	1.9 million	850 thousand	1970	
Washington, D.C.	2.1 million	1146 thousand	1968	7

were always expressed in terms of change in regional share. Population was always divided into four groups, by income, approximating quartiles. These groups are referred to as Lower Income, Lower Middle Income, Upper (or Higher) Middle Income, and Upper (or High) Income.

The five EMPIRIC equation sets were then examined for evidence of consistencies or inconsistencies from one model application to the next. In each application there were, typically, four or five population sectors and five or six employment sectors being forecasted. The precise sectoral definitions differ from one application to the next, but are generally similar.

As above, the population is usually defined as household income quartiles or groups approximating quartiles, while employment usually consists of a few basic and a few non-basic sectors. For each sector, the dependent variables are change in the zone's share of the region's total amount of the particular activity. The independent variables are of four types. First, there are lagged, or base year, values of the dependent variables and second, there are the other dependent variables. The third type of independent variable is the accessibility and/or land use variables of which there are usually several. Finally there are the public utility variables such as sewer and water availabilities.

The general procedure involved in applying the EMPIRIC model involves first, the preparation of a large file of raw (i.e. corrected, but unmodified) and constructed (i.e. combinations or modifications of raw) variables. A selection is then made of variables, generally those which have worked well in prior applications, for use in the preliminary regression analyses. The completion of the model calibration is then a matter of testing alternative variables until a best fit set of equations and parameters is obtained. EMPIRIC is, in a sense, very much an opportunistic model in that the final selection of variables to be used is largely based on the results obtained in the regression analyses. Those variables which produce the best fit being the ones used in the model. The regression fits obtained by this means are generally good, with coefficients of determination ranging upwards from 0.55, many of them being in the range of 0.70 to 0.90.

The measure of goodness of fit used in the EMPIRIC applications was the multiple coefficient of determination R^2. These results are tabulated for the various studies in table 2.4.2. Note that there are two sets of results for most regions. These represent the R^2 from calibration or fitting the model to the data set, and the R^2 from reliability tests. The reliability tests consisted of using the fitted model to forecast the second data point (e.g. 1970) from the first (e.g. 1960) and then comparing the forecast to the actual data (e.g. estimated 1970 vs. actual 1970).

In table 2.4.3 are shown the coefficients of the population variables used in the final versions of the EMPIRIC population equations for each region. A fair degree of consistency is found here, though there are some obvious discrepancies both in sign and magnitude of these coefficients. Note that the coefficients shown are those which were statistically significant, as those which were not significant are not published in the PMM reports.

An interesting pattern shows in table 2.4.3. For each population class, the change in share of a region's total population found in each zone, moves with the change in share of the adjacent population class, viz.; Lower Income moves with change in share of Lower Middle Income, Lower Middle Income moves with change in shares of Lower Income and Upper Middle Income, and so on. Further, for each population class, change in share moves in opposition to (i.e. the signs of the coefficients are negative) its own concentration in the base year and moves with (though the pattern is weaker) concentrations of the next higher income group. Stated in other words, changes in share by zone of each income group move (1) with changes in shares of the next higher and next lower income group, and (2) away from concentrations of their own income group towards concentrations of the next higher income group.

The patterns found in these coefficients of the population variables are quite consistent with hypotheses regarding peoples desires for increased socioeconomic status, as well as with hypotheses regarding peoples unwillingness to live among groups very different from themselves. The patterns of coefficients of other variables in the population equations as

TABLE 2.4.2. Fitting and reliability results – R^2 for several EMPIRIC applications for the four population classes.

Name of region	Number of zones	Time period	Test type	Lower income	Lower middle	Upper middle	Upper income
Atlanta	183	1961–70	Calib.	0.558	0.792	0.812	0.770
	290	1961–70	Reliab.	0.540	0.670	0.810	0.830
Boston	104	1950–60	Reliab.	0.990	0.950	0.915	0.946
	453	1950–60	Reliab.	0.951	0.906	0.793	0.826
Denver	183	1960–70	Calib.	0.647	0.841	0.855	0.839
	"	"	Reliab.	0.938	0.890	0.702	0.694
Puget Sound	244	1961–70	Calib.	0.573	0.719	0.900	0.850
	"	"	Reliab.	0.880	0.816	0.822	0.855
Twin Cities	108	1960–70	Calib.	0.702	0.708	0.812	0.715
	"	"	Reliab.	0.919	0.940	0.880	0.827
Washington, D.C.	110	1960–68	Calib.	0.698	0.770	0.844	0.750
	"	"	Reliab.	0.947	0.917	0.877	0.886

well as those of the variables in the employment equations do not exhibit a similar degree of uniformity, and consequently are not tabulated here, though the specific case of the Twin Cities application is discussed in more detail below.

In the other portions of these EMPIRIC model equations the sense and sensibility of the variables used, and their coefficients is another matter. There are a number of instances of contraintuitive coefficient signs and many constructed variables whose real meaning is somewhat obscure. A harsh critic could assert that the equations derived all their correlations from the unavoidable implicit correlations between activities in urban areas. Thus from the causal point of view the model results could be called fortuitous and/or spurious. A more reasonable position would be that the equation sets depend, to a significant degree, upon these strictly associative relationships, but that they will probably produce reasonably good near term forecasts, taken all together. Another view of these equations is that they are the reduced form of structural equations (in the econometric sense) which are unknown. If this view is correct, as it well may be, the use of these equations for forecasting requires that both the structure and the parameters of the unknown structural equations remain constant over the forecast period. Problems arise, as will be discussed later in this report, when policy tests with this model are attempted by means of changing specific variables. In the absence of a known, or even of an assumed structural form, it is likely that changing variables in the reduced form equations will produce peculiar results. That this concern is justified will be amply demonstrated in the discussion of sensitivity tests of EMPIRIC in a later chapter of this report.

As part of this project the three EMPIRIC applications for which data were available were all run several times, to the end of becoming more familiar with their operation. Of these three, Boston, Washington, D.C., and the Twin Cities, recalibration runs were made for the Boston and Twin Cities data sets. For the Twin Cities data set the equations presented in the PMM final report were rerun using both ordinary least squares (OLS) regression and two stage least squares (TSLS), regression.[1] The differences between the OLS and TSLS calibration reruns were minor, as were all but one of the differences between the PMM calibration and these calibration reruns. The reason for the one larger difference is neither known nor

1. Peat, Marwick, Mitchell and Co. (1971), 'Calibration and Application of an EMPIRIC Activities Allocation Model for the Twin Cities Metropolitan Area', prepared for the Metropolitan Council, St. Paul, Minnesota.

TABLE 2.4.3. Population coefficients in EMPIRIC models.

| | | Population by income (independent variable) | | | | | | | |
| | | Change in share | | | | Base year share* | | | |
Dependent variable	Study area	Low	Lower middle	Upper middle	Upper	Low	Lower middle	Upper middle	Upper
Change in share low income population	Atlanta	−0.119	+0.558	−0.367					
	Denver		+0.129			−0.392	+0.337		
	Washington		+0.229		−0.281	−0.199		+0.258	
	Twin Cities		+0.40		−0.39	−0.42	+0.36		
	Puget Sound		+0.352			−0.314	+0.294		
	Boston		+0.637	−0.295		+0.133		−0.109	
Change in low-middle income population	Atlanta	+0.512		+0.480					
	Denver	+0.201		+0.307			−0.353	−0.334	
	Washington	+0.194		+0.781			−0.279	−0.182	
	Twin Cities	+0.28		+0.45				+0.10	
	Puget Sound			+0.531			−0.054*		
	Boston	+0.53		+0.337			−0.101		

Change in share upper-middle income population	Atlanta		+0.439		+0.338				
	Denver		+0.612		+0.25				
	Washington	−0.14	+0.658		+0.399		−0.27		
	Twin Cities		+0.45		+0.26	−0.16			
	Puget Sound		+0.434		+0.43			−0.219	−0.155
	Boston	−0.125	+0.637		+0.294			−0.224	+0.113
Change in share upper income population	Atlanta		+0.512						−0.447
	Denver	−0.42	+0.685						−0.481
	Washington	−0.507		+0.504					
	Twin Cities			+0.83					
	Puget Sound			+0.657			+0.219		−0.437
	Boston	−0.282		+0.603					−0.278

*Base Year Share

Total Household

important in the context of this project. The differences in coefficients were also minor in all cases. The variable definitions for this EMPIRIC application are shown in table 2.4.4. The statistically significant co-efficients of the equations for the TSLS calibration rerun are given in table 2.4.5. Table 2.4.6 is a comparison of calibrations of EMPIRIC: Twin Cities data.

The great number of constructed variables used in the EMPIRIC equations make it rather difficult to interpret the results of the parameter estimations. There are few consistencies to be found in this parameter set. There are many peculiarities to be mused over. Why is change in a zone's share of population in the low income quartile positively related to change in local

TABLE 2.4.4.   Variables definitions – Twin Cities EMPIRIC

Δ indicates 'change-in-share' variables; all others are base year shares.

LIQ	= Households in lowest income quartile
LMIQ	= Households in lower-middle income quartile
UMIQ	= Households in upper-middle income quartile
HIQ	= Households in highest income quartile
MISC	= Construction and other miscellaneous employment
MFGW	= Manufacturing and wholesale employment
TCU	= Transportation, communications, utilities employment
MFGW	= Manufacturing and wholesale employment
TCU	= Transportation, communications, utilities employment
RET	= Retail employment
SVCFIR	= Service, finance, insurance, real estate employment
LGOVED	= Local government and education employment
HAHU	= Highway accessibility to households
TAHU	= Transit accessibility to households
AHU	= Composite (sum of highway and transit) accessibility to house-holds
HAEMP	= Highway accessibility to employment
AEMP	= Composite accessibility to employment
SEWER	= Percent of district 'sewered'
NCA	= Net commercial area
NIA	= Net industrial area
NPA	= Net public and semi-public area
USEDAC	= Used area = NCA + NIA + NPA + net residential area
VACAC	= Vacant or agricultural area
DEVAC	= Developable area = USEDAC + VACAC
TOTAC	= Total area of the district
TOTHU	= Total housing units
TOTEMP	= Total employment
NRA	= Net residential area

---

*Shares means regional share of variable X to be found in zone

TABLE 2.4.5. EMPIRIC equations for Twin Cities — U. of P. Two Stage Least Squares estimates.*

ΔLIQ $= 0.407\Delta$LMIQ $- 0.377\Delta$HIQ $+ 0.106\Delta$LGOVED $- 0.415$LIQ $+ 0.357$LMIQ $- 0.890\Delta$(HAEMP * USEDAC)
$+ 0.269\Delta$SEWER $+ 0.060$(SEWER * VACAC) $+ 0.112$ (TOTEMP/TOTHU)

ΔLMIQ $= 0.299\Delta$LIQ $+ 0.425\Delta$UMIQ $+ 0.092$UMIQ $- 0.109$(AEMP * USEDAC) $+ 0.300\Delta$(HAEMP * USEDAC)

ΔUMIQ $= - 0.144\Delta$LIQ $+ 0.415\Delta$LMIQ $+ 0.261\Delta$HIQ $- 0.163$LIQ $+ 0.058$ (SEWER * TOTAC) $+ \sim 0.104$ (UMIQ/TOTHU)

ΔHIQ $= - 0.416\Delta$LIQ $+ 0.0\Delta$LMIQ $+ 0.830\Delta$UMIQ $+ 0.248\Delta$SEWER $- 0.260$(HIQ/TOTHU) $+ 0.274$(INDUS/TOTEMP)

ΔMISC $= 0.44\Delta$RET $+ 0.20\Delta$SVCFIR $- 0.026$(TOTEMP/TOTHU) $+ 0.112$(ΔSEWER * TOTAC) $- 0.256$MISC
$- 0.096$SVCFIR $+ 0.109$(NIA * VACAC/(USEDAC + VACAC) $+ 0.094$TAHU)

ΔMFGW $= 0.013\Delta$SVCFIR $+ 0.190$(SEWER * TOTAC) $+ 0.254$SVCFIR $- 0.189$MFGW $- 0.268$NCA
$- 0.531$(USEDAC/(USEDAC + VACAC)) $- 0.248\Delta$HAHU * USEDAC $+ 0.52$HAHU

ΔTCU $= 0.737\Delta$RET $+ 0.919\Delta$SEWER $+ 0.249$NIA * VACAC/(USEDAC + VACAC) $- 0.352$MFGW
$+ 0.60$USEDAC/(USEDAC + VACAC) $+ 0.1827$CU $- 0.53$(TOTEMP)/(NIA + NCA + NPA)
$+ 0.31$(TOTEMP/TOTAC) $- 0.423$(NCA * VACAC/(USEDAC + VACAC))

ΔRET $= 0.473$SVCFIR $+ 0.518\Delta$LMIQ $+ 0.077$NCA * VACAC/(USEDAC + VACAC) $- 0.32$RET
$+ 0.291$AHU * USEDAC

ΔSVCFIR $= 0.169\Delta$UMIQ $+ 0.202$MFGW $+ 0.344$RET $- 0.154$GOVED $- 0.228$SVCFIR $+ 0.236$RET

ΔLGOVED $= 0.29$LΔLIQ $+ 0.313$TAHU $+ 0.214$NCA $- 0.539$LGOVED

*Variables are 1960 share or (for Δ variables) change in share 1960–1970. R^2 for these equations are given in table 2.4.6.

TABLE 2.4.6. Comparison of calibrations of EMPIRIC: Twin-cities data.*

Dependent variable	1 PMM-2^2	2 UoP-TSLS-R^2	3 UoP-OLS-R^2
ΔLIQ	0.702	0.703	0.706
ΔLMIQ	0.708	0.714	0.720
ΔUMIQ	0.812	0.816	0.824
ΔHIQ	0.715	0.715	0.724
ΔMISC EMP	0.750	0.746	0.761
ΔMFG	0.718	0.708	0.714
ΔTRANSP	0.504	0.464	0.464
ΔRET	0.790	0.790	0.793
ΔSERV + FIRE	0.755	0.754	0.758
ΔLOGOV + ED	0.545	0.545	0.546

Column 1 – Resulting R_2^2 from PMM calibrations
Column 2 – Resulting R^2 from this project's recalibration
            using Two Stage Least Squares regression.
Column 3 – Resulting R^2 from this project's recalibration
            using Ordinary Least Squares regression.

*Identical dependent and independent variables were used in all three calibrations.

government and educational employment and negatively related to change in the product of highway accessibility to employment and used land area? Why is change in a zone's share of population in the upper middle income quartile not related to any employment or access variable? Why is change in a zone's share of population in the high income quartile positively related to the base year industrial employment as proportion of total employment in the zone; and not related to any other employment or access measure? More generally why aren't the EMPIRIC variables described as relative values rather than shares, thus avoiding the need to interpret what a zone's share of the percentage of something in the zone implies?

In the absence of an explicit theory or an attempt at structural equations, there can be few expectations regarding signs and magnitudes of coefficients. Consequently there is little point in discussing the EMPIRIC calibration results at length. Suffice it to say, the parameters of EMPIRIC model can be calibrated to yield relatively close fits to the data. The only consistency in the parameters from one application to the next appears in the population group-to-population group relationships. The parameters for other variables and other equations are catch as catch can, and raise questions as to the simultaneity alluded to in the general descriptions of the model which accompany each application. Overall, attempts to use these models for any but short term, no policy, forecasts should be viewed with considerable skepticism.

2.5. ESTIMATION OF A GROWTH ALLOCATION MODEL FOR NORTH-WEST ENGLAND

I. Masser, A. Coleman,
and R. F. Wynn

Environment and Planning, 1971, vol. 3, pp. 451–463

The version of the EMPIRIC model developed for North-west England differs from previous versions in two ways. Firstly, it is designed simply as a means of forecasting changes in population and two broad categories of employment in terms of the zonal shares of these variables. Transportation criteria and possible policy variables, such as public utilities, are largely ignored. This decision reflects the relative scarcity of statistical information for the latter but the simplification of the model is also felt to be justified by the finding in a previous study that 'the non policy variables over which the planner has no direct control, are generally stronger determinants of locational patterns than are the policy variables' (Brand et al. 1967, p. 15).

Secondly, it is designed with a view to utilising published census information as far as possible, since, in the past, one of the major obstacles to the development of models of this type has been the difficulty of gathering time series data for small areas. A satisfactory version of the model developed from published material would considerably widen its range of possible applications in planning studies.

Given the objective of forecasting changes in zone shares of three variables – population, service employment, and manufacturing employment – the specification of the model might take the following more or less general stochastic form:

$$\Delta\text{POP} = \beta_{13}\Delta\text{MAN} + \beta_{12}\Delta\text{SERV} + \gamma_{14}\text{POP} + \gamma_{15}\text{SERV} + \gamma_{16}\text{MAN} + \\ + \gamma_{18}\Delta\text{ACCEMP} + \gamma_{19}\text{AREA} + u_1; \tag{1}$$

$$\Delta\text{SERV} = \beta_{21}\Delta\text{POP} + \gamma_{25}\text{SERV} + \gamma_{24}\text{POP} + \gamma_{27}\Delta\text{ACCPOP} + u_2; \tag{2}$$

$$\Delta\text{MAN} = \beta_{31}\Delta\text{POP} + \beta_{32}\Delta\text{SERV} + \gamma_{36}\text{MAN} + \gamma_{34}\text{POP} + \gamma_{35}\text{SERV} + \\ + \gamma_{37}\Delta\text{ACCPOP} + \gamma_{38}\Delta\text{ACCEMP} + \gamma_{39}\text{AREA} + u_3. \tag{3}$$

This involves the following variables:

ΔPOP   = the change in zonal share of subregional population between times t and $t + 1$.

ΔSERV   = the change in zonal share of subregional service employment between times t and $t + 1$.

ΔMAN   = the change in zonal share of subregional manufacturing employment between times t and $t + 1$.

POP   = the zonal share of subregional population at time t.

SERV   = the zonal share of subregional service employment at time t.

MAN   = the zonal share of subregional manufacturing employment at time t.

ΔACCPOP = the change in zonal share of total accessibility to population between times t and $t + 1$.

ΔACCEMP = the change in zonal share of total accessibility to employment between times t and $t + 1$.

AREA   = the zonal share of subregional land area.

As in previous versions of the model the accessibility variables were estimated as follows:

$$A_i = \sum_j D_j \exp\left(-\beta d_{ij}\right)$$

where

$A_i =$ the accessibility of zone i,
$D_j =$ the population (or employment) of zone j,
$d_{ij} =$ the travel time between zone i and zone j,
$\beta =$ an externally derived constant (in this case 0.185).

The rationale behind the specification set out in equations (1), (2) and (3) can be summarized as follows:

1. Changes in a zone's share of population and manufacturing employment are mutually determined population movements may be expected to follow new employment opportunities created by manufacturing industry, while changes in the latter may be influenced by the relative availability of labor and local markets. Both these variables may also be influenced by changes in the distribution of service employment which in its turn, will respond to changes in population shares.

2. The values derived for the three endogenous variables which express changes in shares may be proportional to the level of these shares at the start of the time period over which the change takes place. This proportional relationship can also be extended to include the initial shares of other variables. In the case of population it is postulated that changes are also related to the share of both service and manufacturing employment; the share of population is included in the case of services, and shares of both population and service employment for manufacturing.

3. Accessibility to other zones, as described above, may influence movements of population and employment. Zonal changes in population shares may be influenced by changes in the relative accessibility of that zone to centers of employment. Similarly, zonal changes in manufacturing and service employment shares may be influenced by changes in the relative accessibility of that zone to centers of population. Because of interindustry linkages, zonal changes in manufacturing may also be influenced by changes in the relative accessibility of that zone to centers of employment.

4. Area may be considered as a possible influence on changes in zonal shares of population and, perhaps to a lesser extent, manufacturing employment in view of their demands on land resources. . . .

Ordinary least squares estimates of the alternative structural equations of the model

Although the application of ordinary least squares (OLS) in the estimation of a simultaneous equation model leads to biased parameter estimates even for infinitely large samples, it is more convenient to use for the purpose of preliminary tests of significance before moving to an appropriate estimation procedure such as two-stage least squares (TSLS). The estimates obtained from the two procedures should not be too dissimilar. Significance is discussed in terms of:

1. 't-ratio' estimates for individual parameters (these being the ratios of estimates to their calculated standard errors);
2. estimates of the F-statistic as a measure of the significance of the fit of each equation as a whole to the observations;
3. the coefficient of determination $\bar{R}^2$ adjusted for degrees of freedom, which is an estimate of the proportion of the variation in the dependent variable associated with variation of the explanatory variables;

4. the estimated variance of the disturbance term for each equation $(\hat{\alpha}_u^2)$.

It should be noted that strictly speaking the ratios of estimated slope parameters to their estimated standard errors do not have the t-distribution for a simultaneous equation model. They are approximately normal, however, and large values may therefore be used as an indication of statistical significance, especially when a large sample is available. Similar conclusions, of course, apply to the use of the F-statistic. The determinant (CD) of the matrix of estimated zero-order correlation coefficients for each equation is also given as an indication of the presence of multicollinearity.

The first and third equations may not be estimated in the form given above without reducing the number of explanatory variables by one and two respectively. There are thus a number of possible just-identified variants of these equations. Fortunately, these variants include all those equations which have just those variables found to be significantly associated with the dependent variables. If the variables which appear not to be significant at the 1 percent level of confidence are dropped the result is as follows:

ΔPOP	Constant	ΔMAN	ΔSERV	POP	SERV	AREA
	0.0673	0.2692	0.3205	−0.1354	0.06210	0.02347
	(5.29)	(6.17)	(3.92)	(11.1)	(3.97)	(4.91)

F	$\overline{R}^2$	$\hat{\sigma}_u^2$	CD
94.1	0.864	0.00483	0.0583

$$(4)$$

ΔSERV	Constant	ΔPOP	SERV	POP	F
	0.0198	0.3814	−0.1715	0.1569	169
	(1.02)	(3.51)	(21.3)	(13.0)	

$\overline{R}^2$	$\hat{\sigma}_u^2$	CD
0.874	−0.00893	0.150

$$(5)$$

ΔMAN	Constant	ΔPOP	MAN	POP	ΔACCEMP
	−0.0598	0.7340	−0.07956	0.1238	0.7881
	(1.95)	(3.96)	(2.82)	(4.38)	(3.10)

F	$\overline{R}^2$	$\hat{\sigma}_u^2$	CD
19.9	0.509	0.0205	0.0394

$$(6)$$

The number of variables in the model is reduced to eight as Δ ACCPOP is not found to be significant in any of the equations. Equation (4) is therefore now just-identified while the other two equations are over-identified. As might have been anticipated, the last equation proves to be the worst fit to the data, indicating that a large proportion of the variation in changes in zone shares of manufacturing employment are associated with variables other than those explicitly included in the specification of the model. Each of the jointly dependent 'change variables' are negatively related to levels established for those variables at the start of the observation period. This is presumably a reflection of the tendency for population and employment to become dispersed in the area, so that the shares of the large centers are declining. The change variables are all positively related to each other. Area is shown to be significantly associated only with the dependent variable Δ POP, although it is also significantly related to Δ MAN at the 10 percent level of confidence.

The significance of Δ ACCEMP in the last equation rather than Δ ACCPOP is perhaps surprising, especially when it is not found to be significant in the first equation. As noted earlier, however, the data employed for these two variables may not be appropriate to the study in hand. There is also the possibility that the significance of this variable relates to the concentration of the development of new manufacturing industry in centers, such as industrial estates, which provide the required infrastructure and which exploit inter-dependencies between firms and industries.

The estimation of the first and third equations is complicated by the presence of multicollinearity among the variables. This may be suspected from the values of the determinants of the matrices of zero-order correlation coefficients (which have a value of one if the estimated correlation between each pair of explanatory variables is zero), and from inspection of the matrix of estimated zero-order correlation coefficients of the variables of the model. Close correlation between a pair of variables will mean that their separate influences may not be estimated with confidence. This effect will be evident in the instability of a regression coefficient when a closely correlated variable is dropped and, in extreme cases, by high variances for parameter estimates and, therefore, low values for t-ratio estimates. Some of these effects are evident in the first equation with respect to the variables Δ SERV and SERV. Although the variables as a pair are significant at the 1 percent level of confidence, neither is so significant when the other is omitted from the equation, and their respective regression coefficients are subject to considerable change when the other variable is omitted. It seems, therefore, that they should be included, or omitted, as a pair. If they are left out the result is:

Δ POP	Constant	Δ MAN	POP	AREA
	0.0881	0.2579	−0.09083	0.02562
	(6.96)	(5.88)	(18.1)	(4.94)

F	$\bar{R}^2$	$\hat{\sigma}_u^2$	CD	
126	0.837	0.00582	0.972	(4a)

The resulting equation is thus almost entirely free of multicollinearity, although there is some shift in the estimated parameter for POP as a result of the relatively high correlation between POP and SERV. It it is considered that the place of Δ ACCEMP in equation (6) has no *a priori* foundation; then the maximum number of variables which may appear in any equation (if it is to be identified) is reduced to five, in which case Δ SERV and SERV may not both be present in equation (4). The variable Δ ACCEMP may thus be regarded as the identifying variable for the pair of variables Δ SERV and SERV in equation (4). One alternative formulation to the model in the form of equations (4), (5), and (6) would thus be the equations (4a), (5), and

Δ MAN	Constant	Δ POP	MAN	POP
	−0.0670	1.012	−0.1235	0.1731
	(2.07)	(5.88)	(4.77)	(6.98)

F	$\bar{R}^2$	$\hat{\sigma}_u^2$	CD	
20.8	0.448	0.0230	0.0685	(6a)

It is also possible to have a 'halfway house' between these two specifications of the model, in the form of equations (4a), (5), and (6). As specified in equations (4), (5), and (6), the model is not segmentable and all three 'change variables' are mutually and simultaneously determined. In the form of the equations (4a), (5), and (6a) or (6), the model is segmentable: Δ POP and Δ MAN are mutually determined without the influence of Δ SERV which is determined once Δ POP and Δ MAN are established. In the second form the model is also 'only just simultaneous' because the removal of one of the change variables as an explanatory variable in equations (4a) or (6a) renders it recursive when OLS estimation methods may be applied without producing biased estimates. However, there seems no theoretical or empirical justification for dropping either of the change variables in equations (4a) or (6a) (the simple correlation coefficient for ΔPOP and ΔMAN is only 0.320, but it should be remembered that this is obtained from a large sample).

Before moving to the results obtained from TSLS estimation, one or two further points need to be noted about the multicollinearity, and its effect in the three alternative specifications of the model. Equation (4) without the variables ΔSERV and SERV is free of multicollinearity but equations (5) and (6) are both severely affected by this problem, for all the explanatory variables in the respective equations, save ΔACCEMP in equation (6), are closely related one with another. The problem is most serious for ΔPOP and POP in equation (5) and for the same pair of variables plus (a) ΔPOP and MAN and (b) POP and MAN in equation (6). The result is that little confidence can be placed on the estimates of parameters for these variables, as they take on considerably different values depending on whether certain variables are explicitly included in or excluded from a given equation. Indeed, it is difficult to say what is the correct model in these circumstances. This is not to say that the results obtained are worthless, however, for if the aim of the exercise is to produce predictions for the dependent variables rather than estimates of parameters, then multicollinearity will be no problem if we include all those variables found to be significant, and the relationship between the explanatory variables remains the same in the forecasting period as in the observation period. Sound forecasts may be made even if it is impossible to assess the separate influences of the independent variables, provided these variables continue to be associated with one another in the same way.

The problem of multicollinearity is made considerably worse by the use of predicted values (ΔPÔP, ΔSEÊV, and ΔMÂN) for the change variables (from the reduced form equations) in the place of the original values of these variables wherever they appear as explanatory variables in the structural equations of the model . . . .

The model specified in equations (4a), (5) and (6a) is especially badly hit by these problems. In this case the association between these variables is so close, while the zero-order correlation between ΔPOP and both ΔSERV and ΔMAN is so reduced, that ΔPOP is not a significant variable in equations (5) and (6a) where ΔPÔP replaces ΔPOP. The predictions of ΔMAN from the reduced form equations are so poor ($\overline{R}^2 = 0.217$) that the substitute variable ΔMÂN in equation (4a) is found to be significant only at the 25 percent level of confidence, even though ΔMÂN is unrelated to either POP or AREA.

Somewhat better TSLS results are obtained for the model as specified in equations (4), (5), and (6):

ΔPOP	Constant	ΔMAN	ΔSERV	POP	SERV	AREA
	0.0544	0.2932	0.5372	−0.1635	0.1016	0.02166
	(2.98)	(3.18)	(2.34)	(5.66)	(2.56)	(3.74)
	F	$\hat{\sigma}_u^2$	CD			
	64.9	0.00663	0.00862			

$$(4)$$

ΔSERV	Constant	ΔPOP	SERV	POP	F	$\hat{\sigma}_u^2$
	0.00721	0.4836	−0.1702	0.1649	158	0.00948
	(0.28)	(2.75)	(20.0)	(10.1)		
	CD					
	0.0734					

$$(5)$$

ΔMAN	Constant	ΔPOP	MAN	POP	ΔACCEMP
	−0.0143	0.2830	−0.06701	0.07759	1.086
	(0.29)	(0.68)	(2.05)	(1.60)	(2.95)
	F	$\hat{\sigma}_u^2$	CD		
	13.2	0.0250	0.0116		

$$(6)$$

For the 'halfway-house' specification mentioned earlier, that is, equations (4a), (5), and (6), the reduced form equations of course remain the same as for the above specification, and the estimation results for equations (5) and (6) are the same. The results for equation (4a) are:

ΔPOP	Constant	ΔMAN	POP	AREA	F	$\hat{\sigma}_u^2$
	0.0883	0.2881	−0.09070	0.02531	98.6	0.00711
	(6.31)	(3.93)	(16.3)	(4.39)		
	CD					
	0.961					

$$(4a)$$

The main effect of multicollinearity for specifications using equations (4/4a), (5), and (6) is in equation (6). Here only ΔACCEMP remains significant at the 1 percent level. Generally, however, the results from this model are close to those obtained earlier for OLS estimates. They again show that the change variables are positively related with one another, while there is a negative correlation between the change variables and the corresponding variables for initial shares. Nevertheless, the estimated parameters need to be regarded with considerable caution. For instance, the parameter estimate for POP, which is highly correlated with SERV, changes from -0.1635 in equation (4) to -0.0907 in equation (4a). The principal value of the estimated model must therefore be viewed in terms of its usefulness in predicting the three jointly dependent change variables.

For this purpose two alternative formulations of the reduced form equations of the model may be used: (a) the reduced form equations as estimated by OLS in the first stage of the TSLS procedure, or (b) reduced form equations obtained from solution of the TSLS estimated structural form equations above. In the first case any unexplained variation is minimized but the restrictions on the structural form equations (5) and (6) are ignored. If it is believed that these *a priori* restrictions are valid, then the second statement of the reduced form equations should be used. If the OLS estimated reduced form equations are found to give better forecasts, then this is some indication that the restrictions are incorrect . . . .

Conclusion

The results from this preliminary test of models of the EMPIRIC type against English data seem promising, although difficulties were experienced in the use of published material and the results are far from conclusive. In particular, the specifications of the model adopted suffered from serious multicollinearity and little confidence can be placed in parameter estimates. This problem is an inherent weakness of the model, at least as applied to this particular region, and there is little that can be done about it, say, by means of a respecification of the model. It should also be emphasised that these models are concerned only with growth allocation and the reliability of estimates of absolute rather than relative changes would also depend on the accuracy of predictions of overall subregional growth. However, within the limitations set by these matters, the model may prove a valuable means of forecasting.

Although some difficulties were experienced in respect of the published information that was available, the study suggests that models of this type can be successfully developed from these sources, which broadens the range of their possible applications in planning studies. Another interesting, although incidental, result of the study is to be found in the OLS estimates. If Δ MAN is treated as an exogenous variable in the model then it reduces to equations (4a) and (5), which is a simple recursive model that can be estimated to predict the change in shares of population and service employment without experiencing problems of multicollinearity to the extent noted. In view of the current interest in models of the Lowry type, which start from the hypothesis that basic employment can be estimated exogenously, the possibilities of this simple allocation model may be worth more detailed consideration.

Appendix

Definition of variables

ΔPOP	=	The change in zonal share of subregional population between 1961 and 1966.
ΔSERV	=	The change in zonal share of subregional service employment between 1961 and 1966 (SIC order 17–24).
ΔMAN	=	The change in zonal share of subregional manufacturing employment between 1961 and 1966 (SIC order 1–16).
POP	=	The zonal share of subregional population in 1961.
SERV	=	The zonal share of subregional service employment in 1961 (SIC order 17–24).
MAN	=	The zonal share of subregional manufacturing employment in 1961 (SIC order 1–16).
ΔACCPOP	=	The change in zonal share of total accessibility to population between 1961 and 1966.
ΔACCEMP	=	The change in zonal share of total accessibility to employment between 1961 and 1966.
AREA	=	The zonal share of subregional land area.

References

Brand, D., B. Barber, and M. Jacobs, 'A system technique for relating transportation improvements and urban development patterns', Report prepared for 46th meeting of the Highway Research Board, Washington, D.C., 1967.

Christ, C. F., *Econometric Models and Methods*, John Wiley, New York, 1966.

Hill, D. M., 'A growth allocation model for the Boston region', *Journal of the American Institute of Planners*, 31, pp. 111–120, 1965.

Hill, D. M., D. Brand, and W. B. Hansen, 'Prototype development of statistical land use model for Greater Boston region', *Highway Research Record*, no. 114, pp. 51–70, 1966.

Traffic Research Corporation, 'Calibration report: Empiric land use forecasting model 97 subregion version', report prepared for the Massachusetts Metropolitan Area Planning Council, Boston, Mass., 1966.

2.6. THE CONSTRUCTION OF AN URBAN GROWTH MODEL

David R. Seidman

Delaware Valley Regional Planning Commission
Report Number 1, Technical Supplement, vol. A
(No date, circa 1970)

The residential location model – RESLOC

The structure of the model

The residential location model, called RESLOC, and the manufacturing location model, called LINTA, have exactly the same mathematical form. They are given different names simply to remind the user that different variables are used in each. Their common mathematical form was originally called LINT, standing for *Linear Int*eraction Model (although the model as a whole is non-linear). It is constructed to project the number of households of a given type, or the number of manufacturing employees of a given type, located in a specified district at the end of a five-year period. This location is considered to occur in two stages.

First, the amount of the locating activity – for example, the number of households – is assumed to increase in each district in the same proportion as the overall regional increase during the five-year time period.

Second, these households are considered to *relocate* in certain amounts from less desirable to more desirable districts. The amount of relocation from one district to another is stated to be in proportion to the difference in the 'desirabilities' of the two districts. The desirability of each district is the sum of the independent variables multiplied by their parameters.[1]

LINT is a trend model. It works with the rate of change of distribution of an activity over time; it assumes that there is a lag between the time a household *should* move, neglecting moving costs, if it is to be in its best location, and the time that it actually does move. Thus, the residential and manufacturing activities are assumed to be located in a somewhat non-optimal manner. Therefore, if one fixed the position of everything which affects the location of the activity, it would continue to redistribute itself for a while until it finally approached a stable equilibrium distribution. Since in the running of the model the influencing factors are never entirely fixed from

---

1. That is, they are in linear combination of the independent variables weighted by their parameters.

one period to another, the locating activities never actually achieve an equilibrium position.

The non-linear regression technique ... was used to obtain parameter valves for each of the dependent variables. (The dependent and independent variables are described in the next section.) ... the linear regression technique estimates the parameter values non-applying to the independent variables in a separate run for each dependent variable. No simultaneous solution over all dependent variables is involved.

The LINT model can be stated in four equations described below. Each equation will first be described verbally and then mathematically.

1. The number of households located in a given district at the end of a specified recursive period is equal to the number of households there in the beginning of the period, plus the rate of change of households in the district, times the duration of the period.

$$\hat{R}_j = R_j + T\dot{R}_j, \tag{1}$$

where

j = a subscript normally designating the district being projected
$\hat{R}_j$ = the estimated number of households in district j at the *end* of a time period
R_j = the number of households in district j at the beginning of a time period
$\dot{R}_j$ = the rate of change in the number of households in district j during a time period
T = the duration of a time period.

2. The rate of change in the number of households in a district is equal to the growth rate of the number of households of that type in the region, plus the algebraic sum of the rates at which households migrate between the district being considered and the other districts in the region, in units of households per year.

$$\dot{R}_j = \sum_{k=1}^{n} (\Delta_{kj} - \Delta_{jk}) + pR_j \tag{2}$$

where

k = a subscript normally designating a district other than the one
being projected

Δ_{jk} = the number of households per year relocating from district j to
district k during a time period

p = the regional growth rate of households of a given type during a
time period.

3. The number of households relocating per year from one district to another is proportional to the number of households in the district moved from, the effective land area of the district moved to, and the difference in the 'desirabilities' of the two districts. No movement is considered to occur from a more desirable district to a less desirable one.

$$\Delta_{jk} = R_j E_k \cdot \text{Max}\left[0, (H_k - H_j)\right] \qquad (3)$$

where

E_k = the effective area of district k
(See the discussion of the independent variables for the definition
of this variable.)

H_j = desirability (i.e. attractiveness) of district j for the locating activity
at the beginning of a time period.

4. The desirability of a district with respect to the activity being located is the sum of the independent variables measured on the district, weighted by their parameters.

$$H_j = \sum_{h=1}^{m} a_h X_{hj} \qquad (4)$$

where

a_h = the parameter defined for independent variable h
X_{hj} = the value of independent variable h in district j
m = the total number of independent variables.[2]

This concludes the description of the four equations which compose the LINT model. In order to use these equations in calibration and projection, it is necessary to bind them into an efficient computational form.

The dependent and independent variables for RESLOC
This section presents the dependent and independent variables used in the residential location model. RESLOC projects the location of households in four separate income classes: 0–$4,000 per year, $4,000–$7,000, $7,000–$10,000, and $10,000 or over. These income class levels are defined as of 1960. For later years the boundary values are recomputed . . . .

Separate projections by income class are made for two reasons. First, the locational behaviors of the income classes are markedly different from each other. Moreover, a universally rapid rise in income will cause large shifts in the proportion of households falling in each income group. Thus, projecting the aggregate location of households without differentiating among income groups might seriously distort these locational forecasts.

Second, estimates of 1985 median incomes by district are required in the automobile ownership model in the transportation simulation process . . . the preferable method of projecting median income by district is by use of income classes.

The independent variables used in the final version of RESLOC are:

1. Proportion of households with income greater than $7,000 (in the upper two income classes).
2. Net residential density.
3. Weighted accessibility measure for RESLOC.
4. Proportion of available land (with a maximum value of 0.6).
5. Proportion of manufacturing and storage land.

One further variable which must be inputed into the model is the effective area, denoted in the mathematical write-up by the symbol E. As stated in equation (2) of the previous section, migration into a district is considered to be proportionate to its effective area. We first defined effective area to be total useable land. However, because there was too much migration to the farthest outlying district in our first projections from 1960 to 1965, we redefined the effective area to be the minimum of either the quantity: residential plus vacant land at the beginning of the period; or the quantity:

---

2. Note that neither the relocation rate, Δ_{jk}, nor the desirability, H_j, is a measured quantity. They are intermediate variables used to derive the theory, and are neither independent variables used as input nor dependent variables to be compared with available data.

2 × residential land at the beginning of the period.[3] This definition was chosen because an analysis revealed that very rarely does the amount of residential land in a district more than double during any given five-year period. It was therefore assumed that the area germane to the migration of households into the district could be no larger than twice the amount of residential land existing in the beginning of the period. A subsequent analysis caused us to redefine the effective area for Dependent Variable Number 1, households with 0–$4,000 income, to be the effective area as defined above, multiplied by the net residential density.

Displayed in table 2.6.1 is a matrix providing the final Beta parameter value applying to each of the independent variables for each of the dependent variables. Included are the R^2 values, the measures of the model's ability to predict the values of each dependent variable.

TABLE 2.6.1   RESLOC parameters (Betas).

Independent variable	Dependent variable	Households with income $		
		0–4000	4–7000	7–10,000	10,000+
1. Proportion of households over $7000		0.05	0.04	−0.03	0.22
2. Net residential density		−0.09	−0.25	−0.34	0.29
3. Weighted accessibility* for RESLOC		−0.005	−0.07	−0.27	−0.39
4. Proportion of available land		−0.03	0.13	0.54	0.92
5. Proportion of storage land		−0.04	−0.03	−0.03	−0.06
R^2		0.993	0.975	0.938	0.910

*Inaccessibility.

A brief history of the calibration of RESLOC, the residential location model

This historical account is included to give the reader who is unfamiliar with model development effort a better idea of the process involved and the types of issues and decisions which occur.

Because of the lack of definitive studies on the subject, we greatly overestimated the power of component analysis to assist regression analyses in

3. (4 × residential land) for the 10-year period used in the calibration runs.

achieving stable and meaningful parameters when highly collinear variables are involved. Thus, our first calibration attempt for RESLOC used 18 dependent variables and 60 independent variables. The parameters obtained were highly unstable, varying radically according to the number and the ranking of components chosen to go into the model. Also, there were both high negative and high positive parameter values assigned within sets of collinear variables, such as the various accessibility measures. The only way to get the parameter values on similar variables to be weighted in the same direction was to take so few components that practically no differentiation could be found between *any* variables. Similarly, the parameters for specific independent variables varied widely and randomly across the different dependent variables.

For these reasons a second set of calibration runs was specified, in which the dependent variables were reduced to eight, consisting of households by race and income; and the independent variables were condensed from 60 to 24. Generally, three criteria were used for selecting the new set of independent variables. First, variables which were extremely collinear were either aggregated or dropped. Generally speaking, we much preferred to aggregate variables rather than to drop them. Our reason for this was the belief that two variables which are correlated presently might become less correlated in the future; thus using both of them serves as a hedge to avoid the more extreme predictions which might result from using only one variable or the other. Furthermore, if policy variables are involved, using both variables assures that the model is sensitive to a wider variety of policies. For example, even though transit and auto accessibilities are highly correlated, it is desirable to include them both so that the model can be affected by both transit and highway policies. Of course, if one has a strong intuitive notion that one variable has a more basic causal relationship to the dependent variable than the other, then the latter should be dropped.

The second criterion we used was that variables which were intuitively significant were retained unless they behaved highly irrationally. This is in accordance with the assertion made in the previous paragraph.

Finally, variables which seemed to have significant values for most of the dependent variables were kept.

Parameter irrationality and instability appeared in these calibration runs also, although not as markedly as in the first set. During the time the calibrations were being done on the 24 independent variables, several projection runs were made as well, projecting from 1960 to 1985. There were very marked differences in the projections made with the different sets of parameters obtained for the different sets of components used in the calibration runs. It was therefore decided that further aggregations and deletions of the variables were necessary. The accessibility measures were weighted together.... Other aggregations and deletions were made until only eight independent variables were defined. The dependent variables were aggregated to four household classes stratified by income.

Other modifications were made to the calibrations at this time as a result of trial projection runs for 1960–1965. These runs projected far too much growth in the peripheral areas of the region. The calibration area was therefore extended from the cordon area to the entire nine-county region, and the effective area was changed from total useable land to its present definition (described in the previous section). Additional tests among the eight independent variables finally narrowed the choice down to the five used in the final calibration run. Each of the calibration sets in the final series was used to produce a projection from 1960 to 1965, and each result was map-plotted and evaluated. These projections were extremely similar to each other, which contrasts with the projections obtained using 24 independent variables. This suggested that even though the parameters themselves still showed instability, the projections are probably reasonably stable.

Since the 1965 population estimates used to check the projection results contained considerable error themselves, and since the 1965 projection results were quite close to each other, these projections could not be used to select between the various sets of variables and components used in calibration. It was also interesting to notice that the residual errors occurring during calibration were generally reproduced during projection. Since these errors tended to cluster together geographically, we suspect that the model contains some systematic error caused by the exclusion of one or more significant variables or the choice of incorrect forms of some of the included variables. Discovery of some of these systematic errors would improve the predictive power of the model.

The computational form of the residential location model
Let us first define the symbol δ_{jk} (delta) such that:

$$
\begin{aligned}
\delta_{jk} \quad &= 1 \qquad \text{if} \quad H_k - H_j \; > \; 0 \\
&= 0 \qquad \text{if} \quad H_k - H_j \; \leq \; 0
\end{aligned} \tag{1}
$$

Then:

$$
\begin{aligned}
\delta_{jk} \quad &= 1 - \delta_{kj}, \qquad k \neq j \\
&= 0, \qquad\qquad\quad k = j
\end{aligned} \tag{2}
$$

Equations (2), (3) and (4) of section 1 can now be combined as follows:

$$\dot{R}_j = \sum_{k=1}^{n} \left[R_k E_j \delta_{kj} (H_j - H_k) - R_j E_k \delta_{jk} (H_k - H_j) \right] + pR_j$$

$$\tag{3}$$

$$= \sum_{k=1}^{n} \left[R_k E_j \delta_{kj} + R_j E_k \delta_{jk} \right] (H_j - H_k) + pR_j$$

To construct a simpler form, let us now construct the following new dependent variables:

$$Y_j = \dot{R}_j - pR_j \tag{4}$$

Then:

$$Y_j = \sum_{k=1}^{n} \left[R_k E_j \delta_{kj} + R_j E_k \delta_{jk} \right] (H_j - H_k) \tag{5}$$

Substituting equation (4) of section 1 into equation (5) above:

$$Y_j = \sum_{k=1}^{n} (R_k E_j \delta_{kj} + R_j E_k \delta_{jk}) \left[\sum_{h=1}^{m} a_h (X_{hj} - X_{hk}) \right]$$

$$\tag{6}$$

$$= \sum_{h=1}^{m} a_h \sum_{k=1}^{n} (R_k E_j \delta_{kj} + R_j E_k \delta_{jk}) (X_{hj} - X_{hk})$$

Now let us define a new set of independent variables, Z_{hj}:

$$Z_{hj} = \sum_{k=1}^{n} (R_k E_j \delta_{kj} + R_j E_k \delta_{jk}) (X_{hj} - X_{hk}) \tag{7}$$

so that Y_j can be computed as:

$$Y_j = \sum_{h=1}^{m} a_h Z_{hj} \tag{8}$$

Using equations (1) of section 1 and (4) above, we can compute $\hat{R}_j$ in terms of Y_j, R_j and T as follows:

$$
\begin{aligned}
\hat{R}_j &= TR_j + R_j \\
&= TY_j + TPR_j + R_j \\
&= TY_j + (1 + pT)R_j
\end{aligned}
\tag{9}
$$

Since the values of the δ_{jk}'s depend upon the H_j's, and these in turn depend upon the parameters, a_h, the set of least squares parameters must be solved for by an iterative process in which the Z_{hj}'s are recomputed for each new set of parameters. It is in fact the dependence of the δ_{jk}'s on the a_h's which makes RESLOC a non-linear model; otherwise it would be a multiple linear regression.

We can now focus on the computation of the partial derivatives of Y_j and $\hat{R}_j$ with respect to the parameters, and on an efficient means of representing the Z_{hj}'s.

The parameters a_h change the values of the Z_{hj} only by changing the ranking of the districts according to the H_j's. Thus, there is a small region around the values of each of the parameters within which the parameters can change values without disturbing the values of the Z_{hj}'s. The partials of Y_j and $\hat{R}_j$ with respect to the parameters are therefore given simply as:

$$
\frac{\partial Y_j}{\partial a_h} = Z_{hj}
\tag{10}
$$

$$
\frac{\partial R_j}{\partial a_h} = TZ_{hj}
\tag{11}
$$

To compute Z_{hj} most efficiently, let us rework equation (7) as follows:

$$
\begin{aligned}
Z_{hj} &= \sum_{k=1}^{n} (R_k E_j X_{hj} \delta_{kj} + R_j E_k X_{hj} \delta_{jk} - R_k E_j X_{hk} \delta_{kj} - R_j E_k X_{hk} \delta_{jk}) \\
&= E_j X_{hj} \sum_{k=1}^{n} R_k \delta_{kj} + R_j X_{hj} \sum_{k=1}^{n} E_k \delta_{jk} \\
&\quad - E_j \sum_{k=1}^{n} R_k X_{hk} \delta_{kj} - R_j \sum_{k=1}^{n} E_k X_{hk} \delta_{jk}
\end{aligned}
\tag{12}
$$

Now let us rank the districts in the order of the values of their desirabilities; so that $H_g < H_{g+1}$. We will define new areal subscripts which are in this order, replacing j by g and k by f.

Translating the first term of (12) into the new subscripts, we have:

$$Z_{hg}^{(1)} = E_g X_{hg} \sum_{f=1}^{n} R_f \delta_{fg} \tag{13}$$

We know from the definition of δ in equation (1) that if $g = 1$, then $\delta_{fg} = 0$ for all f. That is, since district number 1 is the least desirable district, there is no migration into it. If $g = 2$, then $\delta_{12} = 1$, and all other $\delta_{j2} = 0$, etc.

This can be seen in the matrix below of δ_{fg}:

		1	2	3	4	g 5	6	7	...	n
	1	0	1	1	1	1	1	1		1
	2	0	0	1	1	1	1	1	...	1
	3	0	0	0	1	1	1	1		1
f	4	0	0	0	0	1	1	1		1
	5	0	0	0	0	0	1	1	...	1
	6	0	0	0	0	0	0	1		1
	7	0	0	0	0	0	0	0		
	.		.		.		.			
	.		.		.		.		.	
	.		.		.		.			.
	n	0	0	0	0	0	0	0		0

δ_{fg} matrix

If we define the summation in (13) as:

$$S_g^{(1)} = \sum_{f=1}^{n} R_f \delta_{fg}, \tag{14}$$

we can see from the matrix that:

$$S_g^{(1)} = \sum_{f=1}^{g-1} R_f \tag{15}$$

and thus we have the recursive relationship:

$$S_g^{(1)} = S_{g-1}^{(1)} + R_{g-1}, \tag{16}$$

$$S_0^{(1)} = 0$$

Similar recursive relationships can be developed for the other three summations employed in equation (12), using the matrix of δ_{fg} and the fact, from equation (2), that:

$$\delta_{gf} = 1 - \delta_{fg} \quad f \neq g$$
$$= 0 \quad\quad f = g$$

Thus:

$$S_g^{(2)} = \sum_{f=1}^{n} E_f \delta_{gf} = \sum_{f=g+1}^{n} E_f = S_{g-1} - E_g,$$

$$S_0^{(2)} = \sum_{f=1}^{n} E_f = \sum_{j=1}^{n} E_j; \tag{17}$$

$$S_g^{(3)} = \sum_{f=1}^{n} R_f X_{hf} \delta_{fg} = \sum_{f=1}^{g=1} R_f X_{hf} = S_{g-1} + R_g X_{hg},$$

$$S_{h,0}^{(3)} = 0; \tag{18}$$

$$S_g^{(4)} = \sum_{f=1}^{n} E_f X_{hf} \delta_{gf} = \sum_{f=1}^{g-1} E_f X_{hf} = S_{g-1} - E_f X_{hf},$$

$$S_{h,0}^{(4)} = \sum_{f=1}^{n} E_f X_{hf} = \sum_{j=1}^{n} E_j X_{hj}. \tag{19}$$

3. The evolution of Lowry derivative models

3.1. INTRODUCTION

The readings in this chapter all, with one exception, focus on Lowry or Lowry derivative models. The number of applications of these models is rivalled only by those of EMPIRIC. Considered in terms of potential for continued planning application, models of this type, especially when considered in terms of Wilson's entropy maximizing approach, have no serious rivals.

The first reading in this set, by Swerdloff and Stowers describes tests of early, rudimentary, allocation models. Of particular interest are the alternative formulations considered, and the fact that measures of access show up as important explanatory variables.

The second reading is from Lowry's principal description of the model concept and its implementation.

The remaining readings trace the main evolutionary steps in the development of the Lowry derivative models up to, but not including the Wilson entropy derivations. This group is led by Goldner's prose outline of the evolution of the derivative models. The reading by Crecine describes the development of the TOMM model. This is followed by a further reading by Goldner describing the PLUM model. The set is concluded with an excerpt from the CREUE's description of BASS.

In the following pages, prior to the excerpted readings, the evolution of these models and their formulations is described in some detail. This work is based on both published descriptions of the models as well as on careful examination of their expression as computer programs.

3.2. LOWRY DERIVATIVE MODELS

What the name Hershey has become to the chocolate candy bar, the name Lowry has become to the models discussed in this section. All of these models are based on the same basic notion as to how urban-spatial-

processes may be described. While the models differ widely in their treatment of various aspects of the process, in their levels of spatial and sectoral
disaggregation, in the specific forms of the functions used in different
parts of the models, and in their solution algorithms, they all depend on
the same basic notions of urban spatial dynamics originally propounded
by Lowry.[1]

The Lowry model

The numerous versions of the Lowry model and the various models derived
from the Lowry construct comprise the largest class of urban simulation
models. The essence of the Lowry construct involves the projection of a
long-run equilibrium spatial distribution of population and certain types
of employment as a consequence of a predetermined distribution of other
types of employment and assumptions about the behavior of urban
trip-makers. In general the procedure involves use of the locations of
'basic' employment and assumptions about 'work-trip' behavior to
generate a spatial distribution of the residences of the 'basic' employment
employees. Both these spatial distributions, i.e. 'basic' employment and
their residences, along with assumptions about 'shopping-trip' behavior
are used to generate a spatial distribution of 'non-basic' employment.
The locations of the residences of the 'non-basic' employment employees
are then generated by use of the 'work-trip' assumptions for a second time.
The solution of the model thus proceeds in an iterative fashion through
successive allocations of residences and 'non-basic' employment until
either an equilibrium or a 'stopping-point' for the algorithm is reached.

In his work on this model, Lowry considers retail trade, personal
services, entertainments, local schools and government services, and all
other 'local-serving' employment as being 'non-basic' and therefore
endogenous to the model. The 'basic' employment includes such non-
local serving activities as steel-mills, various types of manufacturing,
wholesale trade, and federal government facilities, all of which are predetermined, exogenous inputs to the model. The population in the Lowry
model is not disaggregated, except spatially, with population being treated
as a homogeneous group.

Since this review covers residential location models only, the remainder
of this discussion of the Lowry model deals only with the residential
component of the model. This household allocation function in the Lowry

1. Lowry, I. S., *A Model of Metropolis*, RAND Corp., Santa Monica, Calif., 1964.

model is quite straightforward, being solely a function of accessibility to employment.[2] The function used is:

$$N_j = g \sum_i (E_i / T_{i,j})$$

where

N_j = number of households living in zone j
g = a scale factor (constant)
E_i = number of employees employed in zone i
T_{ij} = a function of the distance between zone i and zone j.

This allocation is subject to two exogenous constraints. First, the sum of all households in all zones must equal a regional total. Second, the density (as households/acre) must be below certain predetermined zonal levels.

Lowry used travel data from the Pittsburgh Area Transportation Study to fit a declining exponential function for work trips. Expressed in terms of probability of a trip of a particular length, the function used in the model is:

$$P_{i,j} = (r_{i,j})^{-1.330}$$

where

P_{ij} = the probability of a work trip being made from origin i to destination j
r_{ij} = the straight line (radial) distance from or g n i to destination j.

In the actual model, according to Lowry, things are less straightforward

... square-mile tracts within the study area were grouped into annuli which are normally concentric on the origin, and one mile in width. The functions shown were evaluated at one-mile intervals, and trips from the origin were allocated among annuli in proportion to these values. The share of all trips received by each annulus was then divided equally among all tracts contained in the annulus.[3]

In the model a matrix of denominators of the population allocation function is computed first. This is done as follows:

$$T_{i,j} = (D_{i,j})^{1.33} R$$

2. Lowry, op. cit. p. 11.
3. Lowry, op. cit. p. 86.

where

$T_{i,j}$ = the denominator of the population allocation function
$D_{i,j}$ = the straight line distance from the origin ($i = j = 0$) to a point i miles vertical distance from the origin and j miles horizontal distance from the origin.
R = the number of zones in an annulus $D_{i,j}$ miles from the origin.

Using Lowry's numbers, for a 6 square mile area, the $D_{i,j}$ matrix is shown first.

Vertical Distance = I							
6	6	6	6	6	7	8
5	5	5	5	6	6	7
4	4	4	4	5	6	6
3	3	3	3	4	5	6
2	2	2	3	4	5	6
1	1	2	3	4	5	6
0						
	0	1	2	3	4	5	6

Horizontal Distance = J

The values of $D_{i,j}$ are shown in the matrix, e.g. $D_{2,4} = 4$. Next the numbers of zones in annuli must be counted as per the following (remember only one quadrant of annulus is shown above, see below):

Distance from origin ($D_{i,j}$)	Number of zones
1	1
2	8
3	16
4	20
5	24
6	40

The annuli can be approximated in a grid system as shown on the following page. It now becomes possible to calculate a new matrix of the denominators of the potential function. These values, the $T_{i,j}$ in the Lowry allocation function, are calculated using the $D_{i,j}$ matrix and the numbers of zones in each approximate annulus. We note that this procedure is, in reality, a way of avoiding the storage of large matrices of travel indices.

5	4	4	4	4	4	5
4	3	3	3	3	3	4
4	3	2	2	2	3	4
4	3	2	1	2	3	4
4	3	2	2	2	3	4
4	3	3	3	3	3	4
5	4	4	4	4	4	5

With this information, a matrix of $T_{i,j}$ is created, which looks rather like the $D_{i,j}$ matrix in configuration:

6	433.	433.	433.	433.	478.	762.
5	204.	204.	204.	433.	433.	478.
4	126.	126.	126.	204.	433.	433.
3	69.	69.	69.	126.	204.	433.
2	20.	20.	69.	126.	204.	433.
1	1.	20.	69.	126.	204.	433.
0						
	0	1	2	3	4	5	6

The need to perform these calculations, in this fashion, resulted from the limits of computer technology when the model was first developed. Current computer technology obviates the need for such gyrations, but the fact that the early models were developed under such restraints is an important consideration when one evaluates their evolution. This example serves to illustrate the type of difficulty which faced the pioneers in urban simulation models.

What remains to be done then is calculate the actual population potentials. This is done as follows. First, the zone for which the potential is being calculated is defined to be a relative origin. Then, for all zones, taken one at a time, the vertical and horizontal distances from the relative origin are calculated. These distances specify an element of the $T_{i,j}$ matrix above, which is divided into the zone's employment. The sum of the results of these divisions, taken over the entire region, is the population potential of the zone. The actual population allocated to each zone is then just a scaling constant times the population potential for that zone. Exogenously supplied maximum density constraints are applied to the population allocation, with any excess population merely being reallocated to other zones in proportion to their population potentials.

Finally, there are some miscellaneous points to be covered here. First, the Lowry model generates a not-quite-instant metropolis. Given the spatial distribution of basic employment, the model's allocations of population and non-basic employment represent an equilibrium situation which would eventually come-to-pass if all other factors remained constant while the equilibrium was being achieved. As such, the model does not purport to be an actual forecasting procedure in as much as it is not possible to associate points in time with either the intermediate iterations, or the solution. Nevertheless, the model provides useful insight into the 'urban-spatial-processes' and opens the way to a great deal of further research on this topic.

The TOMM models

One of the first Lowry derivative models, and one of the most substantively significant, was the Time Oriented Metropolitan Model.[4] This model, developed by Crecine, was also intended for use in Pittsburgh and was to have been a key component of a large, comprehensive, model system. Unfortunately, the contract was terminated before the model system was completed and, for that matter, before TOMM was calibrated. Nonetheless, prototype versions of the model were tested and the substantive differences between this model and its progenitor are important and worth discussing.

First, and most important, was the fact that TOMM was an incremental model rather than an 'instant-metropolis' model. In the TOMM model, which was intended for projection purposes, the base year distributions of *all* activities are included as determinants of the projection year's distributions of activities. The essential notion here is that, in contradistinction to the original Lowry model, not all households nor all 'non-basic' employ-

---

4. Crecine, J. P., 'A Time-Oriented Metropolitan Model for Spatial Location', *Technical Bulletin* no. 6, Community Renewal Program, Department of City Planning, Pittsburgh, Pa., January 1964.

ment is 'free' to move in any given projection period, regardless of its length e.g. 5 or 10 years. Second, rather than treating population as homogeneous, the TOMM model disaggregates population into several types.

Referring first to the original TOMM model, the total household allocation function is rather simple, being strictly a function of access to employment. This allocation is embedded in a more complex process which should be described. First the land available for reallocation is calculated for each tract (zone). This is simply the total land minus, the sum of exogenously determined land use and the stable proportions of residential and commercial land use. As in the Lowry model, commercial land use is assumed to be preemptive vis-a-vis residential land use. Consequently, once the reallocable commercial land is calculated, the remaining reallocable land is for residential purposes.

The actual residential allocation in the model is done in terms of residential densities. That is, using Crecine's notation:

$$N_{j,t}^{H*}/A_{j,t}^{H*} = g \sum_{i} (E_{i,t}/Y_{i,j})$$

where

$N_{j,t}^{H*}$ = Total number of households in zone j at time t
$A_{j,t}^{H*}$ = Total residential land in zone j at time t
g = a scaling factor (constant)
$E_{i,t}$ = total employment in zone i at time t
$Y_{i,j}$ = trip index between zones i and j.

Note that:

$$N_{j,t}^{H} = N_{j,t}^{H*} - N_{j,t-1}^{H*}$$
$$= \text{number of reallocated households in zone } j \text{ at time } t.$$

Analogously:

$$A_{j,t}^{H} = A_{j,t}^{H*} - A_{j,t-1}^{H*}$$

There are several constraints which operate:

1. A constraint on maximum density.
2. A minimum households constraint, corresponding to the stable households.

3. A constraint on the total number of households in the region, to which the sum of the zones is scaled by the factor g.

The model first calculates a residential density allocation for each zone and scales their sum to the regional total. Then the stable households (minimum) constraint is applied. Then a maximum residential density constraint is applied, with any excess being reallocated to all other tracts in proportion to their existing allocations.

The third important difference between TOMM and Lowry is that in addition to disaggregating households, TOMM uses a measure of amenities, albeit very much simplified, to determine the distribution of household types. In particular, given the total numbers of reallocated households per zone, the number of households of each type in each zone is postulated to be a function of the base year number of households of that type, and household specific work trip propensities. The equation is:

$$N_{j,t}^{H1} = r_j \left[p_1 N_{j,t-1}^{H1*} + w_1 \sum_i (E_{i,t}/Y_{ij}) \right]$$

where $N_{j,t}^{H1}$ = number of reallocated households of type 1 in area j at time t and where p_1 and w_1 are exogenously determined constants, and r_j is a scale factor such that the sum of all household types in a zone equals the total households in the zone (as previously estimated). The model then passes to the calculation of the 'non-basic' employment allocations.

At a somewhat later date TOMM was slightly modified with respect to the allocation of household types within tracts.[5] The household specific work trip propensities were deleted. Again, given the total numbers of reallocated households per zone, the number of each household type in each zone was postulated to be a function of the numbers of each household type which were in that zone in the base year. The equation is (using the above notation):

$$N_{j,t}^{H1} = r_j \sum_k (p_{1,k} N_{j,t-1}^{Hk*})$$

where $p_{1,k}$ is a matrix of household-type-to-household-type attractiveness indices. The investigation of this household type specific calculation was

5. CONSAD Research Corporation, 'Impact on Allegheny County Due to the Relocation of Residential and Commerical Activity in the East Street Valley', prepared for Department of City Planning, Pittsburgh, Pa., March 1967.

carried further in another effort.[6] In this case the numbers of each household in each zone were postulated to be a function of: (1) the numbers of each household type which were in the zone in the base year, (2) the percent that each household type was of the total households in the zone in the base year, (3) population potential for each household type, (4) employment potential. These last two variables are not defined in the reference, but are probably some form of work-trip-accessibility measure. Attempts to calibrate these functions were not particularly successful.

The calculation of $Y_{i,j}$ is considerably simpler in TOMM than it was in Lowry, being strictly a matter of calculating the straight line distance between the centroids of the zones. Various efforts to use TOMM have been attempted from time-to-time. It is also the core of several proprietory models such as SCANCAP, PROMUS, and NUCOMS. In some of these, certain of the model's parameters have been estimated, but no truly rigorous calibration of the model has been undertaken to date.

Several years after the publication of TOMM, Crecine published a description of a more sophisticated version of the model which is referred to as TOMM–III.[7] The principal difference between this model and the earlier version was an enormous increase in the sophistication (and complexity) of the amenities measures used for allocation of households, by type, to zones. While there are other minor differences, they are of no substantive significance. The household types are allocated directly to zones, by type, rather than the two-step process of first allocating total households to zone and then disaggregating, which is used in the earlier versions of TOMM. A trial value of households, by type and zone, is calculated based on the 'stable' households in order to start the model's iterative process. The actual household allocation is a function of ten independent variables.[8] The notation of this function is too complex to be worth repeating here. The variables used, in an additive linear function, to forecast location of type L households in zone I at time t, are:

1. Accessibility to exogenous bureaucratic employment, from zone I
2. Accessibility to exogenous industrial employment, from zone I
3. Accessibility to endogenous commercial employment, from zone I

6. Lee, D. B., Jr., 'Household Disaggregation in Urban Models', paper presented at Regional Science Association Meetings, Cambridge, Massachusetts, November 1968.
7. Crecine, J. P., 'Spatial Location Decisions and Urban Structure: A Time-Oriented Model', Discussion Paper No. 4, Institute of Public Policy Studies, University of Michigan, Ann Arbor, Michigan, March 1969.
8. *Ibid.*, p. 38–39.

4. Housing prices in zone I
5. Percent change of household type L in zone I from time $t - 2$ to time $t - 1$
6. A measure of household demand potential in zone I
7. Index of deterioration of structures in zone I
8. Index of public school facilities in zone I
9. Index of other public facilities in zone I
10. Percentage of region's total households of type L which were in zone I at time $t - 1$.

This is an unusually long list of independent variables and raises strong doubts about the likelihood of ever achieving successful calibration. Crecine asserts that some attempt was made to calibrate portions of the model with data from Lansing, Michigan, but it is evident that much work remained before this model could have been considered as really calibrated.

The PLUM and IPLUM models

Another Lowry derivative model, which has been developed in different forms, is Goldner's Projective Land Use Model.[9] Evolving from the tangle of modelling projects in the San Francisco Bay area, the overall construct of PLUM was exactly like that of the Lowry model. With regard to the population allocation procedure there were the following differences: (1) heterogenous zone sizes, (2) a rather different allocation function, (3) residential land calculated not as a residual, (4) density constraints differently applied. Of these, the allocation function is of particular interest and so is described here in more detail.

Consider the theory implicit in the access-attractiveness types of allocation function used in Lowry type models. First, we are concerned with a set of trip-makers and their work-to-home or home-to-work tripmaking. Taking a particular origin, 'all other variables' being equal, the theory postulates that the trips to any given destination will be a function of the difficulty of reaching the destination and the degree to which that particular destination is capable of satisfying the trip purpose. The difficulty of reaching the destination is expressed in distance, or preferably, travel time and/or cost. The degree to which the particular destination

9. Goldner, W., 'Projective Land Use Model (PLUM)' BATSC *Technical Report 219*, Bay Area Transportation Study Commission, Berkeley, Calif., September 1968.

is capable of satisfying the trip purpose is usually expressed in terms of some measure of attractiveness (amenities) or quantity of attractors located at the destination. Two possible 'other' variables are particularly important and therefore are often included in these formulations. First is the possibility of intervening opportunities for satisfying the trip purpose before reaching the 'intended' destination. Second, and really just a different form of the first, is the possibility of competition amongst alternative destinations. Both of these variables have appeared in various models in different ways.

These access-attractiveness functions may be thus thought of as having two components. The first component is the probability of making a trip, for a given trip purpose, of a particular length (time, cost, distance). The second component is the measure of 'attractiveness' of the destination.

In the PLUM model the probability of making a trip of length t is defined by the function:

$$P_t = (\beta/t^2) \exp (\alpha - \beta/t)$$

where

P_t = the probability of making a trip of length t
α, β = empirically derived constants.

This function is applied in the allocation of residences to annular rings around any given origin. Lowry, in a similar situation, divided the probability by the number of zones in each ring. Goldner followed a similar procedure, first calculating the probability of making a trip from the given origin to a given annulus and then dividing this probability by the number of zones in the annulus. In the Lowry model the number of zones in an annulus were arbitrarily defined by the grid system used. PLUM, however, defined the zones to be included in a particular annulus in terms of their travel time from the given origin. Using three-minute intervals, all the zones 0 to 3 minutes from the origin are in annulus 1, all zones 3+ to 6 minutes from the origin are in annulus 2, etc. This procedure allowed the possibility (which does in fact occur with real data) that there will be some annuli containing no zones. PLUM dealt with this problem by adding the probability of travelling to the 'empty' annulus to the next further 'nonempty' annulus. This is shown in the following example.

We begin with an arbitrary probability function as follows:

Travel time $= t$	Probability of trip of length t
1 minute	0.50
2 minute	0.30
3 minute	0.15
4 minute	0.04
5 minute	0.01
> 5 minute	0.00

Now consider that we shall investigate two zones of origin, Zone 1 and Zone 2. Suppose that around each of these zones we define all other zones to be in time rings, e.g. around Zone 1 there is a ring of zones 1 minute away, a ring of zones 2 minutes away, etc. Similarly for Zone 2 there is also a set of such time rings. It is clear that for most regions, depending upon transport facilities, geography, etc., the numbers of destination zones in say, the 2 minute ring, for different zones of origin will be different. Consider the table below:

Origin Zone	No. of destination zones in ring, t minutes from the origin zone				
	1 min.	2 min.	3 min.	4 min.	5 min.
Zone 1	5	0	3	0	2
Zone 2	2	2	3	1	2

Thus in the 2 minute ring for Zone 1 there are 0 destination zones while in the 5 minute ring for Zone 2 there are 2 destination zones.

In the PLUM allocation algorithm the travel probabilities are associated with travel to rings. The probability of a trip from a given origin zone to a given destination zone is equal to the probability of travelling to the destination zone's ring divided by the number of zones in the ring. Consequently the probability of a trip from Zone 1 to a zone in ring 1 is $0.5/5 = 0.1$ while the probability of a trip from Zone 2 to a zone in its ring 1 is $0.5/2 = 0.25$. When a destination ring contains 0 zones the probability of travelling to that ring is added to the next further ring.

Looking again at our example, from Zone 1 there are 0 zones in ring 2. The Zone 1 probability of travelling to a zone in ring 3 is $(0.30 + 0.15)/3 = 0.15$. Summarizing the PLUM calculations for our example:

Origin zone	Probability of trip to dest. zone in ring				
	1	2	3	4	5
Zone 1	0.5/5	n.a.	(0.3 + 0.15)/3	n.a.	(0.04 + 0.01)/2
Zone 2	0.5/2	0.3/2	0.15/3	0.04/1	0.01/2

PLUM then takes this matrix of trip probabilities and normalizes the result across rows of the matrix, producing a final matrix of trip probabilities. This last matrix is used in the final allocation of residences. There is no measure of zonal attractiveness in PLUM, and these probabilities are simply applied to the zonal employments to produce the distribution of residences.

A later version of the PLUM model, hereafter referred to as IPLUM, had an incremental construct.[10] The basic employment inputs were in the form of changes from the base year to the projection year and all the projected allocations were in terms of changes from the base year. These changes were added to the base year variables to produce the future year projections. The allocation function in IPLUM was based on the same exponential function as was used in PLUM, but used in a somewhat different way. In the IPLUM algorithm the emphasis seems to be on intervening opportunities and the probability of travelling from a given origin zone to a given destination zone is equal to the probability of travelling to the destination zone's ring divided by the time to the ring. Consequently using the same numbers as in the PLUM example, the probability of a trip from Zone 1 to a zone in ring 1 is $0.5/1 = 0.5$ and the probability of a trip from Zone 2 to a zone in its ring 1 is also $0.5/1 = 0.5$. Again, with rings containing 0 zones, the entire probability for the 0 ring is added to the next further ring. Thus, since there are 0 zones in Zone 1's ring 4, the probability of travelling from Zone 1 to a zone in ring 5 is $(0.04 + 0.01)/5 = 0.01$. Summarizing the IPLUM cal-

10. Goldner, W., et al. 'Projective Land Use Model' (in three volumes), Institute of Transportation and Traffic Engineering, University of California, Berkeley, California, March 1972.

culations for our example:

Origin zone	Probability of trip to dest. zone in ring				
	1	2	3	4	5
Zone 1	0.5/1	n.a.	(0.3 + 0.15)/3	n.a.	(0.04 + 01)/5
Zone 2	0.5/1	0.3/2	0.15/3	0.044	0.01/5

Both in PLUM and in IPLUM the measure of 'attractiveness' of the destination is basically a measure of residential holding capacity. Using Goldner's notation:

$$O_h(i) = a_v(i)\left[\frac{h(i)}{a_r(i)}\right]$$

where

$O_h(i)$ = number of opportunities for new residential development in zone i

$a_v(i)$ = vacant acreage in zone i

$a_r(i)$ = residential acreage in zone i

$h(i)$ = number of housing units in zone i.

In running of the model, base year values are used to construct the measure. While this is a very simple measure of 'attractiveness', it is probably better than having no measure at all. It does, however, demonstrate a particular inadequacy which Goldner later tried to remedy. This measure, in zones with great quantities of vacant land, tends to substantially overestimate residential development. Goldner used a modification to this attractor function to attempt to correct this tendency. Basically the modification was an attempt to operationalize the notion that developability of land in a zone is related to the existing level of development in that zone. This relationship was intended to be indicative of the operation of infrastructure as an aid to development. The function used, for each zone, was:

$$G(x) = (1 - e^{-3x})/(1 - e^{-3})$$

where

$G(x)$ = index of developability, and $O \leqq G(x) \leqq 1$

X = fraction of usable land already developed in the zone.

This function is introduced simply by multiplying $O_h(i)$ by $G(x)$, before multiplying $O_h(i)$ times the trip probabilities.

Having calculated the opportunities measure, these are used to weight the trip probabilities. These weighted trip probabilities are then applied to the zonal employment increments to produce the zonal population increments – the zonal increments are then added to the base year values to produce the projected new population.

An interesting flaw in the model should be noted here as a matter of general interest. The model, as discussed above, is designed to respond to changes in the location of basic employment and to changes in transportation facilities. Clearly one possibility for basic employment is that there will be no change. The model cannot operate under this condition. This is due to the models describing residential location as a 'net' phenomenon rather than as several components including endogenous intra-urban relocation of residences. Other models, described below, attempt to deal with this problem.

The BASS model

Another model which can be discussed under the rubric 'Lowry derivative', is the residential model from the Bay Area Simulation Study – BASS.[11] While this model is reasonably well known, the precise nature of its workings are rather obscure and not well reported in the literature.[12] One rather complete description of a specific version of the model does exist.[13] Using this in conjunction with a copy of the BASS-IV computer program, it has been possible to decipher its workings.

11. Center for Real Estate and Urban Economics, *Jobs, People and Land: Bay Area Simulation Study* (BASS). Special report No. 6, CREUE, Institute of Urban and Regional Development, University of California, Berkeley, 1968.
Recht, J. R., 'Bay Area Simulation Study: Residential Model', *Annals of Regional Science*, vol. 2 no. 2, December 1968.
12. Stevens, B. and W. Wheaton, Jr., 'A Review of Available Land-Use Activity Distribution Models', Technical Memorandum TM-4524 System Development Corporation, Santa Monica, California, January 1970 (p. 7).
Brown, H. J., J. R. Ginn, et al., *Empirical Models of Urban Land Use: Suggestions on Research Objectives and Organization*, Exploratory Report 6, National Bureau of Economic Research, New York pp. 60–67, 1972.
13. Bernard, C. K., 'The BASS V Residential Model: Exposition, Development, Experimentation, Critique', unpublished Master's thesis, Graduate School of Business Administration, University of California, Berkeley, July 1970.

The essence of the residential allocation in this model is rather simple. The difficulties arise from extensive use of constructed variables and the fact that the calculations are embedded in a large, complex, model system. Briefly, the potential demand for housing is the product of an accessibility measure and a measure of the potential supply of housing. The development of the accessibility measure is described first. The accessibility measure used is that of residence to workplace, but it is developed in a multi-step procedure.

First, the measure of employment by area used in the further calculations is a weighted, and subsequently normalized, function of base year employment and the employment increment. In equation form, this is:

$$\hat{E}_i = a(E_{i,t-1} / \sum_i E_{i,t-1}) + b(\Delta E_i / \sum_i \Delta E_i)$$

where

$E_{i,t-1}$ = total employment in area i at time $t-1$.
ΔE_i = exogenously provided estimate of change in total employment in area i from time $t-1$ to time t.
a, b = parameters, presumably derived from actual data, whose sum is 1.0
$\hat{E}_i$ = employment measure for area i.

This employment measure is, in turn, used in conjunction with an estimate of the supply of housing to construct a further measure which is referred to by various names at different points in the CREUE and Bernard writeups. The measure is sometimes called a distributed weighted employment measure and is later used in another constructed variable incorporating this one and which is called an accessibility measure.[14] Elsewhere the measure $\hat{E}_i$ is called the 'proportion of total housing demand employed in tract i'.[15] The intent or meaning of this measure simply is not anywhere clearly stated. Its calculation includes a declining linear function of inter-areal travel time, and includes only those zones which are found within 50 minutes of the zone for which the measure is being calculated. The calculation is as per the following:

$$E_i' = \hat{E}_i \sum_j [S_j(a + bD_{ij})]$$

14. Bernard, *op. cit.* p. 23.
15. CREUE, *op. cit.* p. 260.

subject to:

$$0 < D_{ij} \leqq 50$$

where

E'_i = the desired new measure
S_j = a relative measure of the potential supply of housing in area j
$D_{i,j}$ = the travel time between area i and area j, in minutes
a,b = exogenously supplied parameters such that $a > 0$; $b < 0$ (in BASS-IV, $a = 1.0$, $b = -0.02$).

It should also be noted that it is not clear where the S_j are obtained from and what is their precise definition.

Finally, this measure, whatever its significance, is used in the construction of the 'accessibility to employment' measure. This measure again uses a declining linear function of inter-area travel time and restricts its consideration to areas within 50 minutes travel time of the zone for which the accessibility is being computed. The calculation:

$$A_i = \sum_j \left[(a + b\,D_{ij})\,E'_j \right]$$

where

A_i = area i accessibility to employment
a, b, D_{ij}, and E'_j are as described above.
This measure is used, in turn, to calculate demand potentials in the demand allocation portion of the model.

At this point it should be clear to the reader as to why this model has not been well described in the literature. There seems to be considerable confusion throughout the development of this access measure. And this is not the end of the confounding of the situation. A similar pyramiding of constructed variable upon constructed variable is undertaken to produce a measure of the potential supply of housing by class, type, and area.

All this not withstanding, it is possible to detect a rationale behind the construction of the accessibility. First note that this measure is ultimately to be used in a housing demand calculation. Thus the $\hat{E}_i$ may be considered as a measure of potential demanders of housing, from both existing employees and new employees, who have their place of work in area i. Subsequently, the E'_i may be considered as a measure of the aggregate potential demanders of housing in area i. This demand results from the demanders $\hat{E}_i$ who work in i adjusted by the spatial distribution of the potential supply of housing in areas within 50 minutes travel time of area i. Finally the accessibility measure for any area i is the result of the spatial distribution of the adjusted measure of demanders, again, for all areas within 50 minutes travel time of the area. Thus the accessibility measure is one of accessibility to potential demanders of housing.

The measure of potential supply of housing is also constructed in several steps. The principal computation in producing this measure involves the product of a measure of the relative suitability of land, in the area, for housing, times a measure of the 'holding capacity' of the developable land. The suitability measure involves a normalized measure of existing housing stocks in the area and in the four closest areas. The housing stock measure is then adjusted by the slope of the land in the area and a proxy measure of land value to produce the suitability measure. The measure of developable land includes both vacant and agricultural land as well as land made available by demolitions. This entire 'product' is then modified by an exogenously estimated attractiveness measure and, again, slope. The precise nature of all this calculation is not central to the current discussion, and it suffices, at this point, to say that explicit interpretation is difficult. Hopefully, a notion of what is done may be obtained from the above description.

The measure of potential supply of housing is multiplied by the accessibility measure to obtain what is called the demand potential:

$P_{j,y,t}$ = demand potential in area j for housing in value class y
A_j = accessibility measure for area j
$S_{j,y,t}$ = potential supply of housing of value class y and type t in area j.

This demand potential is then normalized and the result converted to housing demand by tract, this being accomplished by multiplication times exogenously determined regional housing demand. Then, housing demand and housing supply, by tract, are matched. If the tract demand exceeds tract supply, the new housing is set equal to the supply with the excess demand being saved for a subsequent iteration. If the tract supply exceeds demand the new housing is set equal to demand and the supply is decremented. Excess demand from the various tracts is accumulated and subsequently allocated, as if it were an additional amount of regional demand, to any tracts with available housing as above, thus completing the residential allocations.

Despite the fact that much has been omitted, the description of the BASS residential model has required a rather lengthy exposition. This is justified by the pivotal role that this model plays in the stream of development of these models. All the models described prior to this are essentially 'demand oriented'. These constructs develop a measure, or measures, of the attractiveness and/or accessibility of each area and subsequently allocate households to these areas in proportion to the measure(s). There is no consideration in these models of the availability of housing for the locating households.

A few efforts have been undertaken to model the housing market, i.e. the 'supply side' of the problem. Most notable amongst these was the A. D. Little study of the San Francisco housing market.[16] In addition, the Herbert-Stevens model included housing supply as one of the determinants of household location, but (a) did not attempt to generate estimates of housing supply within the model, and (b) was not made operational until just recently.[17] The BASS model, despite its many shortcomings, particularly that of poor empirical support for an extremely long chain of assertions in its theoretical development, was the first operational model to link the 'supply side' to the 'demand side'. As shall be discussed below, even now, half a decade later very few other models have attempted to deal with this rather critical problem.

Before moving on, it should be mentioned that the Lowry model, in various forms, has been implemented for many areas in England[18] as well as for the city of Ljubljana, Yugoslavia.[19]

In one of these models, by Echenique, et al.[20] the original Lowry household allocation function is modified to include available floor space at the destination zone (i.e. zone of residence). The resultant 'demand' for residential floor space if then constrained by available floor space estimated by an exponentially decaying floor space function.

16. Wolfe, H. B., 'Model of San Francisco Housing Market', *Socio-Economic Planning Sciences*, vol. 1 pp. 71–95, 1967.
17. Wheaton, W. C., 'Income and Urban Location: A Study of American Spatial Demand', unpublished Ph.D. dissertation, Department of City and Regional planning, University of Pennsylvania, May 1972.
18. Batty, M., 'Recent Developments in Land Use Modelling: A Review of British Research', *Urban Studies*, vol. 9, no. 2, June 1972.
19. Stubbs, J. R. and Brian Barber, 'The Lowry Model: A Mathematical Method for Forecasting the Distribution of Population and Jobs in an Urban Region', Technical Report 10, American-Yugoslav Project in Regional and Urban Planning Studies, February 1970.
20. Echenique, Marcial, et al., 'A Model of a Town: Reading', Working Paper 12, Centre for Land Use and Built Form Studies, University of Cambridge, England, June 1969.

The Lowry-Wilson formulation

The versions of the Lowry model which are in current use in England are derivations of a form of the model developed by Alan Wilson through application of entropy maximizing procedures.[21] These techniques and many of their ramifications are described in two recent books and thus need not be described again here except for the following brief notes.[22]

Virtually all of Lowry derivative models in the U.S. have as their basic residential allocation function some form of the following expression:

$$N_i = g \sum_j p_{ij} E_j \tag{1}$$

where

N_i = number of residential locators locating in area i
p_{ij} = the probability of living in area i and working in area j
E_j = the number of employees in area j
g = a scaling factor such that the sum of the N_i over all i equals an exogenous control total.

There are often other scaling or multiplier factors to convert from employees to households and to assure internal consistencies of various types.

The most important component of equation (1) is obviously the p_{ij}. It will be recalled that in the original Lowry model, the function used was:

$$p_{ij} = (D_{ij})^{-1.33} R \tag{2}$$

where

D_{ij} = airline distance between the centroids of area i and area j
R = number of zones in an annulus D_{ij} miles from the origin.

It is a virtue (and perhaps in the first instance was the source) of the Wilson entropy maximizing approach to analysis of these models that the question of trips is made explicit. For example, the Lowry model may

21. Wilson, A., 'Development of Some Elementary Residential Location Models', *Journal of Regional Science*, vol. 9 no. 3, December 1969.
22. Batty, M., *Urban Modelling*, Cambridge University Press, Cambridge, 1976. Wilson, A., *Urban and Regional Models in Geography and Planning*, Wiley, London, 1974.

be rewritten based on this approach as:

$$T_{ij} = E_j \, \mathscr{F}(C_{ij}) \tag{3}$$

where

T_{ij} = number of persons working in zone j and residing in zone i
E_j = number of persons working in zone j
C_{ij} = impedance (usually travel time or travel cost) between centroids of zone i and zone j.

An important problem of this formulation is that there is no constraint on the sums of trips. Without the constraint there is no reason to expect that:

$$\sum_j T_{ij} = E_j \tag{4}$$

This implies that the number of employees in zone j will not equal the sum of the employees residing in all zones i who claim to work in zone j.

In contradistinction, a simple residential location model may be derived from entropy maximizing concepts as follows:

$$T_{ij} = A_i B_j O_i E_j \mathscr{F}(C_{ij}) \tag{5}$$

where

T_{ij} = trips between zones i and j or, number of persons living in zone i and working in zone j
O_i = trip origins or, employed persons living in zone i
E_i = trip destinations or, employees employed in zone j.
A_i = balancing factor for trip origins
B_i = balancing factor for trip destinations
$\mathscr{F}(C_{ij})$ = impedance function.

It is possible to replace the trip origins O_i by a measure of attractiveness of the origin zone, W_i. This eliminates the need for the origins balancing factor A_i thus giving:

$$T_{ij} = B_j W_i E_j \mathscr{F}(C_{ij}) \tag{6}$$

In order for the constraint on the sums of trip destinations, equation (4), to be met, we have:

$$B_j = \frac{1}{\sum\limits_i W_i \mathscr{F}(C_{ij})}$$ (7)

It is informative to substitute this expression back into the original equation yielding:

$$T_{ij} = E_j \left[\frac{W_i \mathscr{F}(C_{ij})}{\sum\limits_i W_i \mathscr{F}(C_{ij})} \right]$$ (8)

If the term $W_i \mathscr{F}(C_{ij})$ is called an 'accessibility attractiveness' measure, then the fraction in the above measure is a relative measure of the accessibility-attractiveness of zone i to zone j compared to all other zones i. Further, it is clear that the total number of employed residents residing in zone i is:

$$N_i = \sum\limits_j T_{ij}$$ (9)

and substituting:

$$N_i = \sum\limits_j E_j \left[\frac{W_i \mathscr{F}(C_{ij})}{\sum\limits_i W_i \mathscr{F}(C_{ij})} \right]$$ (10)

This is equivalent to saying:

$$N_i = \sum\limits_j E_j p_{ij}$$ (11)

which is the same function as the Lowry model, described in equation (1) where

p_{ij} = the probability that a person will work in zone j and live in zone i.

This revised Lowry formulation, despite its innocuous appearance has important ramifications, leading to, among others, solutions of the problems of calibrating these models and procedures for linking them directly to transport network packages.

The excerpts that follow trace the development of these models to this point, setting the stage for current applications of these models to planning problems.

3.3. A TEST OF SOME FIRST GENERATION RESIDENTIAL LAND USE MODELS

**Carl N. Swerdloff and
Joseph R. Stowers**

Highway Research Record No. 126 (1966) pp. 38–59
U.S. Bureau of Public Roads

This paper reports on a comparative evaluation of five operational residential land use forecasting techniques, four of which have been previously used in urban transportation planning studies. These techniques are representative of the earliest of efforts in the development of operational urban activity simulation models and continue to serve, either in their original or in modified form, a great number of transportation planning organizations. Urban activity simulation models currently under development, while in most cases considerably more complex and, hopefully, more accurate, in many instances draw upon notions and fundamental concepts which either originated with or were adapted to these early techniques. Improvements being introduced in these later, second generation models include more complex statistical estimating procedures, the stratification of residential locators into several distinct groups, and the incorporation of behavioral relationships in the model formulation. These newer techniques may require several years of research, evaluation and refinement before they become fully operational. Meanwhile, the less sophisticated approaches evaluated in this report should continue to be useful to such smaller metropolitan areas as are lacking the resources for developmental research.

The primary objective of this project was to compare the relative accuracy of these approaches through a series of *ex post facto* tests, holding all conditions constant except the interrelationships among variables, so that differences in 'forecasts' would be a function only of inherent differences in models.

The techniques used were (a) the density-saturation gradient method, (b) accessibility model, (c) regression, and (d and e) two intervening opportunity models.

The density-saturation gradient method (DSGM) is a simplification of the approach used by the Chicago Area Transportation Study.[1,2] Of the five techniques, the DSGM is least computer-oriented, more demanding of subjective inputs, and therefore least suitable for objective comparison with other approaches, particularly when the forecasters are not intimately familiar with the area. The method is based essentially on the regularity of the decline in density and percent saturation with distance from the CBD, and the stability of these relationships through time.

The simple accessibility model is based upon the concept formulated by Walter Hansen.[3,4] Growth in a particular area is hypothesized to be related to two factors: the accessibility of the area to some regional activity distribution, and the amount of land available in the area for development. The accessibility of an area is an index representing the closeness of the area to all other activity in the region. All areas compete for the aggregate growth and share in proportion to their comparative accessibility positions weighted by their capability to accommodate development as measured by vacant, usable land.

The third method used in this study, multiple linear regression, is a popular approach because of its operational simplicity and ability to handle several variables.[5,6,7] The proportion of total regional growth which locates in a particular area is assumed to be related to the magnitude of a number of variables which in some manner are measures of geographic desirability as viewed by those making the locational decision. The procedure is to determine those factors, and their weights, which in linear combination can be related to the amount of growth which has been

1. Hamburg, J. R., and R. H. Sharkey, Land Use Forecast, Chicago Area Transportation Study, 3. 2. 6. 10, August 1, 1961.
2. Hamburg, J. R., Land Use Projection for Predicting Future Traffic, *Highway Research Board Bull.* 224, pp. 72–84, 1959.
3. Hansen, W. G., Land Use Forecasting for Transportation Planning, *Highway Research Board Bull.* 253, pp. 145–151, 1960.
4. Hansen, W. G., 'How Accessibility Shapes Land Use', *Jour. of the Amer. Inst. of Planners*, May 1959.
5. A Projection of Planning Factors for Land Use and Transportation, Baltimore Regional Planning Council, Tech. Rept. No. 9, March 1963.
6. Graves, C. H., The Multiple Regression Models of Small Area Population Change, *Highway Research Record no. 102*, pp. 42–53, 1965.
7. *Hartford Area Traffic Study Report*, vol. 1, Conn. Highway Dept., July 1961.

observed to take place over a past time period. These factors (called independent variables) and their weights (regression coefficients), in linear combination (the regression equation) can then be applied to the individual analysis areas to forecast the magnitude of growth (the dependent variable).

Although more commonly applied to the problem of trip distribution, the intervening opportunities models can be used in simulating the distribution of urban activity. Two separate and distinct formulations were applied in this study, both based upon the general notion that the probability that an opportunity is accepted decreases as some function of the number of opportunities ranked closer to a central distributing point. The Stouffer formulation was originally applied to intra-urban migration.[8] A related formulation has more recently been investigated as a trip distribution technique.[9] Schneider's formulation was originally applied to trip distribution[10] and is currently being used in distributing urban activity.[11,12]

Performance and interpretation of results

Performance
The single accuracy measure which was calculated for all trial forecasts was the sum of squares of dwelling unit forecasting error. These measures were computed at four levels of geographic aggregation: sector, ring, district, and zone, for all trials. A sixth forecast was made using the naive assumption of equal growth for all zones. The error sum of squares computed under this assumption, which will be referred to as the naive model, is $(n - 1)$ times the variance in actual zonal residential growth. It will serve as a benchmark in evaluating the results of the five techniques listed.

8. Stouffer, Samuel A., 'Intervening Opportunities: A Theory Relating Mobility and Distance', *Amer. Soc. Rev.*, vol. 5, no. 6, December 1940.
9. Tomazinis, Anthony R., The Development of the Penn-Jersey Transportation Study Trip Distribution Model, Penn. Jersey Paper no. 15, presented at 41st Annual Meeting of Highway Research Board, Wash. D.C., January 1962.
10. Chicago Area Transportation Study, Final Report, vol. 2, July 1960.
11. Hamburg, J. R., G. T. Lathrop, and G. F. Young, 'An Opportunity-Accessibility Model for Allocating Regional Growth', *Highway Research Record no. 102*, pp. 54–66, 1965.
12. Hamburg, J. R., and G. T. Lathrop, 'An Opportunity-Accessibility Model for Allocating Regional Growth', *Jour. of the Amer. Inst. of Planners*, May 1965.

Table 3.3.1 gives the computed error sum of squares for all of the forecasts and calibrations at each level of aggregation. For sake of complete comparisons, the results of zone level forecasts for each of the models (not for the DSGM) have been aggregated to districts and rings defined both by time and distance from the HVC. Trial one of the DSGM was based on analysis at the level of district as defined by distance from the HVC; therefore results are not shown for districts as defined by time to HVC, and vice versa for trial two of the DSGM.

TABLE 3.3.1   Error sum of squares for all trials [a]

| | | Levels of aggregation | | | | |
| | | Districts | | Rings | | |
Method	Zone	By distance ring	By time ring	By distance	By time	Sector
DSGM						
Trial I	2.33	6.97	–	8.36	–	9.69
Trial II	2.41	–	4.43	–	4.07	3.02
Accessibility model						
Forecast	1.80	4.16	2.84	3.25	2.33	4.58
Fitted	1.79	3.98	2.76	2.18	1.99	4.46
Regression (fitted)	1.85	4.71	3.14	5.16	2.84	3.71
Stouffer model						
Forecast	2.21	6.45	4.22	5.57	3.48	11.25
Fitted	1.91	4.72	3.07	2.42	1.46	8.84
Schneider model						
Forecast	2.07	6.16	4.13	4.10	3.38	13.92
Fitted	1.95	4.65	3.08	1.91	1.65	10.18
Naive model	2.20	7.66	5.22	20.64	10.54	16.18

[a]All values have been multiplied by 10^{-6}.

The sums of square of differences between estimated and actual are analogous to 'unexplained' variances of a statistical model. However, since valid statistical inferences obviously cannot be drawn, this terminology should not be used. The error measurements of table 3.3.1 provide an index which can be used to compare results in any single column, that is, for the same level of aggregation. Comparisons between columns are meaningless, since different numbers of areas and different variances from mean growth rates are involved at different levels of aggregation.

The accessibility model performed substantially better than other un-fitted models at most levels of aggregation; but the fitted Stouffer and Schneider models were quite comparable to the fitted accessibility model. Somewhat surprisingly, the addition of several other explanatory variables in linear regression form did not improve the accuracy.

Results at the sector level are of interest because of the implications for forecasting radial corridor movements. Here the intervening oppor-tunity models yield comparatively poor results, perhaps because they were not made sensitive to the distribution of employment, as were the accessibility model and regression equation.

3.4. A MODEL OF METROPOLIS

I. S. Lowry

RAND Corp., Santa Monica, Calif.
August 1964

The formal model

The Pittsburgh Model is at best a half-way house on the road to a general model of urban form. Its map of the metropolis is filled in partly by hand, and it offers a minimum of detail about the characteristics of land use, population, and economic activity allocated to the various sub-areas. Its properties as a model of change over time are not altogether clear, although it is structurally well-adapted to dealing with incremental changes and lag variables.

At its present stage of development, the model is designed as a set of simultaneous equations whose solution represents an 'equilibrium' in the pattern of land use and in the distribution of employment and popula-tion ..., the amounts and distributions of basic employment and basic land use are determined outside the model; given this information, the model generates appropriate amounts of retail employment and residential population, and distributes these employees and households among the sub-areas of the metropolitan region, assigning land for each use.

The model has no normative interpretation. It is meant to simulate – roughly, to be sure – the actual behavior of households and enterprises in a given institutional setting, when they are faced with given circumstances outside their control, and other given circumstances within their control.

It is possible, nevertheless, to conduct policy experiments by altering various explicit parameters of the model and evaluating the desirability of the resultant changes in solution values.

In the following section, I present the formal logic of the model as a set of simultaneous equations. Subsequently, I describe the computational steps used to solve the system.

The model as a system of equations

The logical structure of the model can be expressed in nine simultaneous equations and three inequalities. These standard components are replicated many times in the complete system. The following notation will be used:

A = area of land (thousand square feet)
E = employment (number of persons)
N = population (number of households)
T = index of trip distribution
Z = constraints.

In conjunction with these symbols, the reader will find the following superscripts and subscripts:

U = unusable (land)
B = basic sector
R = retail sector
H = household sector
k = class of establishments within the retail sector; also defines related class of 'shopping' trips
m = number of classes of retail establishments ($k = 1, \ldots, m$)
i,j = sub-areas of a bounded region, called *tracts*
n = number of tracts ($i = 1, \ldots, n; j = 1, \ldots, n$).

Unspecified functions and coefficients are represented by lower-case letters: a, b, c, d, e, f, g.

Land use

We are given the area of each tract, and the amount of land therein which is not usable by any of the activities with which we are concerned. The remainder of the land in each tract is available for use by basic establish-

ments, retail establishments, and households. All land not otherwise assigned is treated as available for residential use.

$$A_j = A_j^U + A_j^B + A_j^R + A_j^H. \tag{1}$$

Basic sector
For each tract, we are given exogenously the quantity of land used by basic
establishments (A_j^B) and the employment opportunities provided by these
establishments (E_j^B).

Retail sector
Retail establishments are divided into m groups, each of which has a
characteristic production function; the elements of this production function which enter directly into the model are: minimum efficient size of
establishment,[1] number of clients required to support one employee, and
number of square feet of space per employee. Since local consumer demand
provides the market for establishments of this sector, we may treat employment in each line of retail trade as roughly a function of the number of
households in the region:

$$E^k = a^k N \tag{2}$$

The distribution of this retail employment among the square-mile tracts
depends on the strength of the market at each location. Assuming that
shopping trips originate either from homes or from workplaces, the market
potential of any given location can be defined as a weighted index of the
numbers of households in the surrounding areas, and the number of
persons employed nearby.

$$E_j^k = b^k \left[\sum_{i=1}^{n} \left(\frac{c^k N_i}{T_{ij}^k} \right) + d^k E_j \right] \tag{3}$$

This equation could easily be made more general; however, we have
assumed that none but short-range pedestrian trips originate from workplaces, so that the only relevant origins are those in Tract j. Those originating from home are often longer vehicular trips, but the likelihood of a
shopping trip from i to j diminishes with intervening distance. (The variable

---

1. Actually the minimum number of employees per tract; these employees may represent
   more than one establishment of the same type.

T_{ij}^K is a positive function of this distance, fitted from an analysis of home-based vehicular shopping trips.) The coefficients c^k and d^k measure the relative importance of homes and workplaces as origins for a particular type of shopping. Finally, b^k is a scale factor which adjusts the retail employment in each tract to the regional total determined in equation 2.

$$E^k = \sum_{j=1}^{n} E_j^k \tag{4}$$

In this way we determine the amount of employment in any tract for each line of retail trade. The sum of these employment figures plus the quantity of basic employment allocated to the tract is total employment for that tract.

$$E_j = E_j^B + \sum_{k=1}^{m} E_j^k \tag{5}$$

Finally, with the aid of exogenously-determined employment-density coefficients (e^k) for each line of trade, we can determine the amount of land in each tract which will be occupied by retail establishments:

$$A_j^R = \sum_{k=1}^{m} e^k E_j^k \tag{6}$$

Household sector

The region's population of households may be regarded as a function of total employment.

$$N = f \sum_{j=1}^{n} E_j \tag{7}$$

The number of households in each tract is a function of that tract's accessibility to employment opportunities.

$$N_j = g \sum_{i=1}^{n} \frac{E_i}{T_{ij}} \tag{8}$$

The coefficient g is a scale factor whose value is determined by the requirement that the sum of tract populations must equal the total population of the region as determined in equation 7.

$$N = \sum_{j=1}^{n} N_j \tag{9}$$

Constraints
In order to limit the dispersion of retail employment, we impose a minimum-size constraint (Z^k), expressed in terms of employment. If the market potential of a particular location does not justify an establishment above this minimum size, the 'customers' are sent elsewhere

$$E_j^k \geqq Z^k, \text{ or else } E_j^k = 0 \tag{10}$$

In order to prevent the system from generating excessive population densities in locations with high accessibility indices, we impose a maximum-density constraint (Z_j^H). The value of this constraint (number of households permitted per 1,000 square feet of residential space) may vary from tract to tract, as would be the case under zoning ordinances.

$$N_j \leqq Z_j^H A_j^H \tag{11}$$

Finally, the amount of land set aside for retail establishments by equation 6 must not exceed the amount available.

$$A_j^R \leqq A_j - A_j^U - A_j^B \tag{12}$$

Taken together with the accounting relationships expressed in equation 1, this constraint also prevents the assignment of negative values to residential land.

Solution of the system

Ignoring for the moment the three inequalities, one can show that the nine structural equations form an adequately-determined system, whose solution (if it exists) describes an 'equilibrium' distribution of retail activities, and a coordinate 'equilibrium' distribution of residential population. The formal adequacy of this structure is demonstrated below by a count of equations and unknowns in the expanded system. . . .

The problem of time

The model as presented ... and as actually programmed and operated to date has no time dimension. Its iterative sequences are simply convenient substitutes for an analytical solution; they generate an 'instant metropolis.'

The reader is entitled to ask what relationship there could be between such an abstraction and a real-world metropolis whose history is embodied in individual structures and even in whole subdivisions dating from the 19th century. Given that the present form of each metropolis is an outgrowth of its unique past, can this form be approximated by a simultaneous system without lag variables?

Experimental results indicate that the answer is a qualified 'Yes.' The model performs this replicative function correctly in broad outline, but is unreliable in detail. Its failings are quite consistent with what we can observe of the processes and pace of change. Despite the 19th century remnants which are visible in today's metropoli, it is clear that these cities are yet functioning systems whose parts are in some way mutually adapted. There is a constant and equally visible process of land-use succession and functional reorganization of activities within our great metropolitan areas, operating both by demolition of existing structures and street patterns, and by adaptation of old facilities to new uses.

Ideally, a model of metropolis should be a dynamic system with variables whose values continuously change under the impact of external forces and internal momentum. Such models are on the horizon; in the meantime, I believe, experimentation with static models is a necessary preliminary to dynamics. The Pittsburgh Model, moreover, is designed so that it can easily be adapted to semi-dynamic form. Thus, its iterative solution has an interesting resemblance to temporal processes of urban change, although the analogy is not exact.

The 'initial conditions' of a dynamic version of the model might consist of the existing distribution of employment, population, and land use. A change in the level and/or distribution of basic employment, or a change in the structural parameters of the model[2] would provide the motive force for subsequent events. To accommodate such a change, the model re-estimates and redistributes population, with due regard for employment-access and land-use constraints. The next step is the redistribution of sufficient retail establishments to serve the new arrangement of house-

2. E.g. parameters representing labor-force participation rates, zoning laws or other limitations on land use, the efficiency of the transportation system, land-use coefficients for households and enterprises. The possibilities are discussed further below.

holds; this event in turn shifts retail employment locations, calling for a
further redistribution of population in subsequent rounds, until an equilibrium is reached. Thus the solution to each successive iteration of the system
of equations can be interpreted as representing changes over time. And
the model is constructed so that it can easily be taken off the computer
between iterations for insertion of further exogenous changes, these
changes in turn redirecting the system toward a new equilibrium solution.

Another way in which the model can be adapted to dynamic problems
is through incorporating lag variables. There are three parameters which
can be used quite effectively in this way:

1. *Available-Land Constraint*: Equation (1) lists four land-use variables and
   a control total. Two of these variables, A_j^U and A_j^B, are data inputs to
   the model; the values of A_j^R and A_j^H are part of the solution. We may, if
   we desire, hold a quantity of land 'off the market' (as A_j^U) for x iterations,
   then either assign it to A_j^B in order to accommodate a postulated growth
   of redistribution of the basic sector, or make it available for retail and
   residential use. Marginal (e.g. steep-slope) land may be withheld from
   the market until population-potential reaches a certain level, then
   released for development.

2. *Minimum-Size Constraint*: Equation (10) is a constraint which prevents
   the location of a retail establishment in a tract whose market-potential
   is below the level necessary to support an establishment of minimum
   efficient size (Z^k). If early iterations in the solution-sequence develop
   retail uses in a given tract, we may argue that the sunk cost in this retail
   development voids the minimum-efficient-size constraint for x iterations thereafter – so that, even though market-potential for that location
   declines during the later stages of the iteration process, the now 'un-
   profitable' retail outlet remains as a competitor, inhibiting the development of other locations.

3. *Maximum-Density Constraint*: We may argue that the original development pattern of residential land inhibits density charges as population
   potential increases. For example, if Tract i is first developed in detached
   single-family houses, we might set the maximum-density constraint for
   that tract at a level appropriate to that type of development, for a period
   of x iterations.

   Tract j, on the other hand, is currently developed in very versatile
   structures which can easily be converted into efficiency apartments and
   rooming houses; therefore the maximum-density constraint is set high

enough to allow for such conversion at any time that access-potential justifies increasing density.

These are only a few of the possibilities, but sufficient to demonstrate that these parameters are built into the model in such a way that, through them, we can substantially alter the dynamic sequence, and/or the final solution. Moreover, they are adaptable to changes: no functional relations need be rewritten; the bulk of the input data is undisturbed. A change of parameters can be a general change affecting all tracts equally; or the change can apply only to a specific tract.

Moreover, through these same parameters we may apply alternative public policies to particular areas, and observe their consequences – e.g. establish the maximum residential density of Tract j by a zoning ordinance or exclude commercial development from Tract i. It should even be possible to simulate a planned redevelopment project through the alteration of these parameters – all in the context of this iterative series. . . .

Fitting the model

From the very beginning, the design of the Pittsburgh Model was constrained by the resources available for fitting its parameters and for validating its overall structure. Since original field work was out of the question, the model had to be accommodated to existing data-files.

In this respect, we were most fortunate in that the Pittsburgh Area Transportation Study (PATS) had assembled a massive file of small-area data pertaining to land use, household characteristics, and travel behavior for 1958. A supplementary home interview survey was done by PATS for the Bureau of Public Roads in the spring of 1960; it offered additional detail with respect to certain relationships between household characteristics and trip-making. The U.S. Censuses of Population and Housing for 1960 provided independent controls for certain of the sample data in the PATS surveys. Studies of the central business district of Pittsburgh by the City Planning Department and the Regional Planning Association gave important information about this concentration of employment and shopping facilities.

Because the PATS data files were so central to our plans, the model was fit to the PATS study area – 420 square miles centered on Pittsburgh. This area encompassed about 1.5 million inhabitants and 550,000 jobs, including all of the Pittsburgh Urbanized Area as defined by the 1960 Census except for three narrow corridors extending into neighboring counties. It also included some 225 square miles of usable vacant or agricultural land – enough space to accommodate Pittsburgh's growth for several decades.

The process of fitting the model involved a great deal of trial and error. Between the first experimental run and the version presented here, there were five major revisions, each involving alterations in computational routines, changes in structural parameters, and different treatments of input data. For example, hospitals and colleges, as places of employment, were shifted back and forth between the basic and retail sectors; alternative groupings of establishments within the retail sector were tried, each necessitating revision of location parameters and minimum-size constraints; alternative solutions to the boundary problem were explored. In the following pages, I have reported primarily on the present version of the model, but some of its features can only be explained by reference to earlier experiments.

I feel rather keenly the inadequacies of empirical work reported here. Somehow, one's theoretical structures always seem to demand more data and more elaborate analysis of data than can be supplied. In the end, one must look back on a record of rough and dirty estimates, of compromises with the principle of parametric independence,[3] of discoveries made too late and of opportunities foregone. . . .

An appraisal of the model

I should make it quite clear that I do not consider the Pittsburgh Model a finished product, which is usable at this point for any serious practical pur-

---

3. Structural parameters – constants which control the behavior of a mathematical system – can be fit either in the context of the system itself, or independently. Following the first method, one chooses parametric values which optimize the performance of the system as a whole in the context of a given set of data; this is typically the case of multiple-regression models. To test the system as a model with more general applicability, one must operate it with new input data, independent of that used for the original parametric fit. If the model still works – in the sense of yielding good estimates of output variables – one gains confidence that the parameters are truly structural.

But for a model too complex for analytical solution, such best-fit parameters can only be derived by trial-and-error, an expensive and usually impractical method. Moreover, where independent sets of data are not available for subsequent testing of the fitted parameters.

The alternative, used in the present case, is to fit the parameters independently of each other, outside the context of the model. The fitted parameters may then be plugged into the system, and the system applied to whatever data are available. There is no guarantee that such an assemblage of independently-fitted components will function smoothly together; but if they do, at least the performance of the system cannot be dismissed as merely reflecting built-in circularity.

pose. It is at best a prototype with a promising future. Its present value lies mainly in the guide-lines it offers for further research. But even from its present ambiguities, there emerge some valuable insights into the spatial structure of metropolis and the trends of change.

The Pittsburgh Model was designed for eventual use as a tool for metropolitan and regional planning. I have assumed that there is a logic to the spatial arrangement of human activities, a logic which is obscured partly by the intrinsic complexity of the relationships among these activities but even more by the large numbers of interacting elements. My aim has been to simplify and generalize the relationships among the myriad locators, while preserving enough spatial detail to be of use in the broader problems of land-use and transportation planning. The resulting model is exceedingly simple in its structure and data-requirements; even so, it strains against the available data-base and the economic limits of computer use.

In the preceding sections of the report, I have offered for the reader's inspection the logical structure of the model, reviewed the steps followed in applying that structure to a specific body of data, and reported on the behavior of the model in actual operation. Limitations of the data-base forestall rigorous tests of the model's ability to replicate the processes of urban development over time; but the experiments herein reported at least demonstrate that the model responds intelligibly to such data as are available.

Perhaps the best service I can offer to the reader by way of summary is to review what seem to me the most salient findings and their implications:

1. The gravity principle seems to have enough flexibility to comprehend the spatial interactions of a variety of locators, and it requires much less of a data-base than any alternative so far proposed. Given only the barest specifications of the properties of urban space and of the units to be located therein, the model was able to generate quite plausible co-distributions of employment and residential population.

2. The model's distributions of resident household and retail facilities can most plausibly be interpreted as a 'forward' solution; i.e. as the end-point of a presently-incomplete process of relocation which is itself a response to past changes in the location of workplaces and to improvements in personal transportation. If the model is to be practically useful, these implicit dynamics must be formalized and assigned a time-scale.

3. The solution of the model calls for more residents than in 1958 in selected locations near the Golden Triangle. For other parts of the central city – the East End, in particular – the model projects population

losses, with commensurate gains for the low-density fringe. As a continuation of the 1950–1960 trend, such dispersion is plausible, although one might question the magnitude of the redistribution called for by the model.

Judgments on this score must take account of the fact that the postwar years have witnessed a considerable dispersion of workplaces. While the Golden Triangle appears to have held its own (replacing retail with administrative employment), the number of jobs elsewhere in the central city has declined substantially. The pattern of residence generated by the model is closely tied to the 1958 distribution of workplaces—much more closely than the pattern of residence actually prevailing at that date. This difference may reflect a failure of the model to take into account other factors conditioning residential location, even in the 'long run'. But a strong argument can be made in favor of the model solution as indicative of the residential pattern of the future.

4. Although the model is anchored to an existing pattern of 'basic' workplaces, it projects a more symmetrical pattern of residential distribution than was apparent in 1958. Pittsburgh's past asymmetry is largely attributable to the importance of the rivers to its major employers and to the topographical irregularities which constrained the routing of overland transportation. Because of its topography, Pittsburgh is perhaps the least appropriate metropolis in the nation for a model which measures accessibility in terms of airline distance.

But in the age of the automobile, the achievements of highway engineers are nullifying the constraints formerly imposed by topographical irregularity, and the logic of spatial symmetry is asserting itself. The opening of the Fort Pitt Tunnel (1960) as a gateway to the western sector of Allegheny County was a major step in balancing radial accessibility to the metropolitan core, and the implementation of the PATS freeway plans will complete this task.

Granted the likelihood that the projection of greater symmetry will thus be realized, it is nonetheless clear that the Pittsburgh Model's distributive routines are inadequately sensitive to features of the transportation system which are more appropriately viewed as exogenous planning variables than as automatic responses to demand pressures. There exist well-developed techniques for tracing minimum travel-times and distances over a specified transportation network, and such a routine could easily be integrated into the Pittsburgh Model –provided that the user were prepared to bear a formidable increase in computational costs.

5. The Pittsburgh Model has a structural capacity for generating output detail for territorial units as small as a square mile. In experimental work to date, I judge the minimum grain of usable output to be at least four times as large; but the model has been constrained only by the barest specifications of the natural and historical properties of these small areas.

The urban environment is well supplied with unique local features of terrain and with legacies of development (e.g. structures and lot-sizes) which condition future uses. Many of these peculiarities defy generalization. However, they may be imposed, tract by tract, as constraints on the model's projected distributions of population and retail employment.

The most pressing need is for greater specification of the characteristics of vacant land and its availability for development, and for density constraints which reflect existing patterns of structural development.

6. The most interesting result of the model's treatment of retail trade was the similarity of market-potential surfaces based on a variety of trip-distribution functions. This similarity suggests a major economy in programming which would allow greater disaggregation of retail trades than has so far been feasible. Instead of calculating a separate matrix of market-potentials for each retail sub-sector, one could calculate a general matrix of retail market-potentials and use other constraints, specific to each retail sub-sector, to enforce different distributions of employment in these sub-sectors. The minimum-size parameters of the present model could be used in this way as constraints on the sub-sector employment distribution.

Moreover, if these repetitions in the calculation of market potentials (and population potentials) were eliminated, it would be more practical to base the calculation on a fully-specified transportation network as suggested above, rather than on airline distance.

7. The identification of homogeneous sub-sectors of retail trade is difficult under any circumstances, but particularly so when the original database is crude, and at a time when merchandizing techniques are rapidly changing. I have experimented with broad kind-of-business classifications and also with typical-cluster classifications. Using the former method, I found that the model was reluctant to generate focal clusters (i.e. concentrated shopping districts); better results were obtained by the latter method, but the model was thereby prevented from reflecting an important current trend, the selective dispersion of kinds of business which were once unique to the metropolitan central business district.

It would be profitable, I think, to re-examine the classification of retail trade with the aid of a stronger data-base.

8. Model-builders nearly always begin by assuming a data-base of better quality than is in fact available. The original design of the Pittsburgh Model was tailored directly to the data-bank of the Pittsburgh Area Transportation Study, which offered as much small-area detail (particularly about employment) as was available anywhere in the nation. Even so, I was forced to assume an implausible level of reliability for small-area samples, and was severely limited as to the disaggregation of variables either for input purposes or for use in the fitting of parameters. The experience leads me to wonder whether any metropolitan model designed for periodic projections of small-area detail can in practice be furnished with the necessary base of current input data.

The future of metropolitan models

The Pittsburgh Model is only one of a number of current attempts to develop quantitative models of metropolitan spatial structures – perhaps the simplest and least ambitious. Its siblings vary in style, including such diverse approaches as a loosely-articulated system study, an exceedingly formal set of simultaneous equations, an elaborate multi-stage mixture of linear programming and computer simulation, and an accounting system for reconciling detailed judgments about the development prospects of small areas.

While it is clear that the present state of the arts is one of experimentation, there is no reason to anticipate eventual agreement on a single all-purpose model of metropolis. These models are oriented to particular planning problems, ranging from urban renewal to the design of a regional transportation system; each has its unique informational requirements. If nothing else, differences in the relevant time-scales, in the need for geographical detail, and in the available data-base must be reflected in the grand strategy of model-building.

The simulation of complex physical, biological, and social systems has become a very active field of research in the past decade; the most advanced models relating to urban systems are those developed by traffic engineers for network assignments. It is becoming increasingly clear that the development and testing of such models is a long-term process, and that their validity will always be ambiguous. Thus, no one can really assert, after ten years of experiment, that traffic-assignment models provide a mechanically reliable guide for transportation planning. But there can be little doubt that the use of these models as an element in the planning process has enormously increased the planners' understanding of metropolitan transportation problems and forced them to deal explicitly and rigorously with many relationships within the system that were previously glossed over.

We can reasonably anticipate a similar future for the current fumbling attempts to submit other aspects of metropolitan planning to the discipline of the computer. Granted that the model-builders will never be able to simulate accurately all of the relevant features of the urban environment, they can at least go far beyond our present inability to trace system-wide and recursive impacts of major changes in environmental conditions or in public policy.

Perhaps even more important is the fact that in communicating with an industrious but simple-minded computer, all questions and instructions must be meticulously framed. In the process, false issues are unmercifully exposed, and others assume hitherto unsuspected importance. In the development of public policy, as in scientific research, the proper formulation of a question is the most important step in reaching an effective answer.

3.5. THE LOWRY MODEL HERITAGE

William Goldner

Journal of the American Institute of Planners, 1971, vol. 37, pp. 100–110

Descendants of the Lowry Model

In general, Lowry-type models display certain characteristics in common: (1) partitioning of employment into a market-oriented category called population-serving or 'retail,' and a residual termed 'basic,' or site-oriented; (2) the causal system leads from 'basic' employment to residential population to population-serving employment; (3) the population-serving allocation grows out of a multiplier relationship applied to basic employment. However, each descendant makes certain fundamental additions to the Lowry framework.

TOMM (Time Oriented Metropolitan Model), 1964

The earliest revision of the Lowry model was generated in Pittsburgh where the stimulus to make the model operational in the CRP was immediately apparent. The responsibility was undertaken by John P. Crecine, under the aegis of the CONSAD Research Corporation. The published technical report (Crecine 1964) indicates that three major revisions were incorporated:

1. Conversion to a 'marginal allocation model that allows only a portion of the establishments and households to move in a certain period of time, rather than the aggregate, allocative model of Lowry's';
2. Household disaggregation '... by income, housing characteristics, social characteristics, or all three';
3. Limitation of 'the simulation study to locational characteristics within the City's Boundaries. . . .'

In addition, the report mentions that 'the City will be sectored into n census tracts,' shifting the zonal system from the mile-square grid adopted by Lowry.

The implementation of the 'marginal allocation' process was made to depend on location as a primary purpose (Goldner and Graybeal 1965). Their model was designed to test the sensitivity of the commercial and residential allocation system to the exogenous emplacement of a large plant at a specific location.

BASS I had several design features that differed from the parent model. First, it used census tracts rather than grid squares as zones. Second, it generated employees, population, and households (Lowry uses households as a surrogate for population). Third, and most important, many of the parameters which are applicable to the whole system in the Lowry model were disaggregated to individual tract-specific form. Labor force participation rates and land absorption coefficients for residential and commercial allocation reflected the base-year relationships, rather than a systemwide average. These tract-specific parameters were closely related to the layers of development to which the urban region has been subject over time. Thus, close to the center, residential densities are high and family size small, contrasted with the development margin where the low-density suburb with larger families is characteristic.

A fourth change from Lowry was the abandonment of the disaggregation of population-serving employment. In effect, the model traded off this disaggregation in favor of the spatial disaggregation mentioned above.

BASS I was a pilot version and was used for testing the effects of the emplacement of several industrial parks. Out of the experience with this model, a program for improvement and redesign was developed. Graybeal chose to pursue a redesign strategy that generated a composite system of separate models. These are included in parts of BASS III, a non-Lowry system of models (Center for Real Estate and Urban Economics 1968), and reported in other places (Graybeal 1966a; Graybeal 1966b). Goldner organized a revision more consistent with the Lowry framework, which became PLUM (Goldner 1968).

The Garin-Rogers contributions, 1966

A serendipitous contribution to the stream of developments originated with a graduate student, Robert A. Garin, in the planning workshop of Professor Andrei Rogers, during the work on BASS I (Garin 1966). Garin expressed the fundamental Lowry algorithm in vector and matrix format. Using this notation, he demonstrated that the iterative process used by Lowry to generate population-serving employment could be replaced by elementary matrix operations to obtain an exact rather than an approximate solution.

Professor Rogers (1966) provided one additional fillip to this development by adding a time dimension to the input vector. This replaced the static equilibrium solution of Garin with an equilibrium displaying *stationarity*, that is, a distribution that arises after repeated application of an unchanging recursive growth process.

Both of these developments were demonstrated with experimental ten-zone allocations. However, for operational use, there are several problems. First, the Garin formulation does not comprehend the constraints which Lowry imposed. Neither the minimum size constraint for population-serving employment nor the maximum density constraint for residential development was included in the matrix operations. In addition, the inversion of a matrix for a large size zonal system presented problems of computer storage and time-cost that might be bypassed by useful approximations. Finally, Rogers' requirement of constant recursive growth is not always consistent with exogenous growth forecasts reflecting shifting age composition of the population and drifting labor force participation.

CLUG (*The Cornell Land Use Game*), 1966

A parallel development was also taking place in the form of a heuristic game designed to teach planning principles to public officials and students. Professor Allen G. Feldt of the Cornell University Department of City and

Regional Planning saw the need for an instrument to bridge the gap between the complexities of planning expressed in sophisticated mathematical terms and the decision-influencing comprehension needed by senior planning officials and local legislators. Working independently, he devised a game that is analogous to TOMM (Feldt 1966).

The model embedded in the game has several elaborations which extend the conceptual framework of the Lowry model. Residential allocation can occur at four densities corresponding to the scaling of densities from single family upward to large multiple unit developments. Instead of a network, there is emphasis on infrastructure (utilities, local government services, and the like) to guide the configuration of development. There is also a governmental revenue and outlay process which relates to the value of land and improvements. In fact, there is a flow of money passing through the system, starting with bids for vacant land, and for other transactions involving wage payments, retail trade, and provision of goods.

The Lowry causal sequence – starting with infrastructure to basic industry to residents to retail – is clearly embedded in the framework. The hand version of the game was essentially a pedagogical tool, and, in a later version, was supplemented by a short computer program to eliminate hand computations and accounting processes that were necessary for the game to proceed.

A dynamic model of urban structure, TOMM II, 1968

Still using the same model name, TOMM Crecine presented a more completely documented version of his earlier model in 1968. The model enlarges upon the Lowry model and the earlier version of TOMM in several ways: the 'variables ... are of a much more disaggregate nature, the concept of site amenities is introduced, and zoning constraints are explicit' (Crecine 1968). Among the elaborations incorporated into the revised version are: (1) white collar and blue collar workers; (2) several household types; (3) inclusion of the effect of site amenities and economic externalities in determining site valuation; (4) incorporation of effects of density, zoning restrictions, and market imperfections on rents; and (5) recognition of the inertia in the urban locational system that results from the durability of physical property and infrastructure.

These changes are backed by careful theorizing and explicit attention to computer applications. Crecine summarizes:

TOMM is still in a development stage. This version, however, approaches the limits of this particular approach to urban locational phenomena. Further efforts on TOMM should focus on developing an appropriate data base and on the considerable parameter estimation problems. Additional theoretical refinements would appear to have only marginal payoffs (Crecine 1968).

This enlarged version of TOMM is '. . . serving as the spatial-location device in the METRO project as the University of Michigan' (Crecine 1968). The project is attempting to develop more sophisticated operational gaming techniques through which several models incorporating technical formulation of plans and decisions by policymakers are matched and evaluated for disparities (Duke and Burkhalter 1966).

PLUM (Projective Land Use Model), 1968

The line of development that grew out of the experiments with BASS I led to the operational version of PLUM (Goldner 1968). PLUM was implemented to provide the land use allocations and small zone forecasts of population, dwelling units, and employment used by the Bay Area Transportation Study Commission (BATSC). In addition to the modifications mentioned with regard to BASS I, PLUM incorporated several additional concepts:

1. Network times were created by careful generation of minimum time-paths (skim trees) with alternatives for free-flow and peak-hour versions, augmented in both cases by terminal times.
2. The gravity allocation function, which has biases strongly influenced by the sizes of zones in the zonal system and is also deficient for its treatment of short trips, was replaced by a more satisfactory function, the reciprocal transformation in logarithmic form. These allocation functions were disaggregated by three types of trips, work-to-home, work-to-shop, and home-to-shop, and were disaggregated spatially by county, requiring calibration of twenty-seven parameters.
3. An additional variable at place of residence allowed population, employed residents, and dwelling units to form a consistent triad that is linked by three vectors of parameters. Parameters, including population per household, workers per household, and population per worker, were zone-specific (spatially disaggregated) and adjusted to drift through time in conformity with exogenous forecasts of employment and population.
4. The model simulates trips rather than estimating them in correspondence to an accessibility index.
5. Land use accounting includes zone-specific acreage for residential and vacant land, rather than the residual treatment characteristic of the Lowry model and TOMM.
6. Constraints on residential developments accomodate to land capacity

and simultaneously to increased density as the zone is filled. Excess demand exerts pressure on density in relation to density transformation coefficients which are calibrated to cross-section data for each county.

7. Comparative statics is the basis for the generation of time increments which are added to initial conditions data to generate target year forecasts, either on a one-step or a five-year recursive basis.

8. The equation system is solved as a causal chain which is made possible by the substitution of approximations of the multiplier process for the matrix inversion suggested by Garin.

References

Center for Real Estate and Urban Economics, *Jobs, People, and Land: Bay Area Simulation Study (BASS)* (Berkeley, Institute of Urban and Regional Development, University of California), 1968.

Crecine, J. P., *TOMM (Time Oriented Metropolitan Model)*, Technical Bulletin Number 6 (Pittsburgh, Community Renewal Program), 1964.

Crecine, J. P., *A Dynamic Model of Urban Structure*, Santa Monica, Rand Corporation, 1968.

Duke, R. D. and B. R. Burkhalter, 'The Application of Heuristic Gaming to Urban Problems', Technical Bulletin B-52, January, East Lansing, Institute for Community Development, Michigan State University, 1966.

Feldt, A. G., *The Cornell Land Use Game*, Ithaca, Center for Housing and Environmental Studies, Cornell University, p. 4, 1966.

Garin, R. A., 'A Matrix Formulation of the Lowry Model for Intrametropolitan Activity Allocation', *Journal of the American Institute of Planners*, 32, November, pp. 361–364, 1966.

Goldner, W., *Projective Land Use Model (PLUM): A Model for the Spatial Allocation of Activities and Land Uses in a Metropolitan Region*, BATSC Technical Report 219, (Berkeley, Bay Area Transportation Study Commission, 1968.

Goldner, W. and R. S. Graybeal, *The Bay Area Simulation Study: Pilot Model of Santa Clara County and Some Applications*, Berkeley. Center for Real Estate and Urban Economics, University of California, 1965.

Graybeal, R. S., 'A Model for Forecasting Residential Development', *The Regional Science Association Western Section Papers*, pp. 134–139, 1966a.

Graybeal, R. S., *Land Use Report*, Honolulu. Oahu Transportation Study, 1966b.

Lee, D. B., Jr., Models and Techniques for Urban Planning, Buffalo, Cornell Aeronautical Laboratory, Ind., 1968.

Rogers, A., 'A Note on the Garin-Lowry Model', *Journal of the American Institute of Planners*, 32, pp. 364–366, 1966.

3.6. A TIME-ORIENTED METROPOLITAN MODEL FOR SPATIAL LOCATION

J. P. Crecine (1964)

Technical Bulletin No. 6
Community Renewal Program
Department of City Planning, Pittsburgh, Pa.

The model presented below represents an attempt to adapt, rewrite, or otherwise alter a regional land use model developed by Ira Lowry for the Pittsburgh Regional Planning Association.[1] The Lowry model had as its task, the allocation of commercial activity and households to specific areas, given a specified mix of basic industrial activity and activities *exogenous* to the region's economy. Given levels of industrial and exogenous activities located at specified points in the region, the commercial activities and households that were supported by the industrial and exogenous sectors were quantified and located by the model into analysis areas.

The Lowry model:

1. Spatially distributed or allocated *all* residential and commercial land uses during one time period (attempted to reproduce the observed locational characteristics of the Pittsburgh region and did not try to predict them).
2. Treated all households as if they were identical.
3. Considered the region as the analytical unit rather than the city defined by artificial boundaries ('artificial' in an economic sense.)

These three characteristics of the Lowry model are at variance with the needs of a simulation model for land use allocation in the City of Pittsburgh, and as will be pointed out below, necessitate major revisions and adaptations of the model. The nature of the revisions are as follows:

1. In constructing a simulation model of the City of Pittsburgh, we need a dynamic, time-oriented model vs. the static Lowry model. For instance, we know that all households or commercial establishments do not have the opportunity to move every two years, four years, or even every

1. Lowry, Ira S., *Design for an Intra-regional Locational Model*, Pittsburgh Regional Planning Association, September 1960.

ten years. A straightforward application of the Lowry model would implicitly assume that this was possible (by reallocating the entire commercial and residential stocks to analysis areas on the basis of *projections* for the industrial and exogenous sectors). What is needed, then is a *marginal allocation model* that allows only a portion of the establishments and households to move in a certain period of time, rather that the aggregate, allocative model of Lowry's.

2. The urban planner (and most other individuals for that matter) knows that all households are not the same, either with respect to their locational behavior or the economic and social implications of that behavior. Consequently, in order to form a simulation-locational model and have it be as useful (and as accurate in its behavioral assumptions) as possible, households ought to be differentiated by income, housing characteristics, social characteristics, or all three.[2]

3. The desire to limit the simulation study to locational characteristics within the City's boundaries could well cause considerable difficulty. Locational and economic behavior usually pay little attention to artificial boundaries. Unfortunately, the extent to which the boundary issue will affect accuracy cannot be determined until the model has been run. The new model, then, will take cognizance of 'needs' (1) and (2) and 'hope for the best' in handling 'need' (3).

Household sector

The municipality's population of households may be regarded as a function of total employment:

$$N_t^{H*} = \mathcal{F} \sum_{j=1}^{n} E_{j,t} \tag{10}$$

The amount of land available for residential reallocation (A_j^H) varies from tract to tract, the number of households per unit of available land –

2. Due to empirical and computational limitations, the number of household categories that can be handled in a meaningful manner will probably be limited to 6 or 7. It will be advisable, then, to pick that dimension which (a) yields maximum observable differences in locational behavior, and (b) correlates with a great many other attributes and characteristics. Because of the observed differences in work-trip distance propensity between different income-level-social characteristics with income, it would be wise to categorize households by income initially and derive the other relevant characteristics from 'income'. (It may be possible to use other subcategories of income such as race, and owner-renter breakouts).

net residential density – in each tract depends primarily on the accessibility of that tract to employment opportunities:

$$\frac{N_{j,t}^{H*}}{A_{j,t}^{H*}} = g \sum_{i=1}^{n} \left[\frac{E_{i,t}}{Y_{i,j}} \right] \tag{11}$$

or

$$N_{j,t}^{H*} = g \sum_{i=1}^{n} \left[\frac{E_{i,t}}{Y_{i,j}} \right] A_{j,t}^{H*},$$

where

$$A_{j,t}^{H*} = A_{j,t}^{H} + A_{j,T-1}^{H*} \tag{12}$$

and $N_{j,t}^{H} = N_{j,t}^{H*} - N_{j,t-1}^{H*}$ is the number of reallocated households, $(t - 1)$ to (t). Here, g is a scale factor whose value is determined by the requirement that the sum of the tract populations equal the total population of the area – as determined in equation (10).

$$N_{t}^{H*} = \sum_{j=1}^{n} N_{j,t}^{H*} \tag{13}$$

In order to prevent the system from generating excessive densities in certain tracts (locations with extremely high accessibility indices), we impose a maximum residential density constraint (Z_{j}^{H}). The maximum density constraint serves the same function as the price mechanism in a market with limited supply.

In order to keep the system from moving more households out of an area than can reasonably be expected during the analysis period (i.e. reducing the number of households below the minimum possible for period t, $N_{j,t}^{HS}$) we introduce a minimum-number-of-households constraints $(N_{j,t}^{HS})$. The minimum households constraint corresponds to residential immobility. The constraints operate through the scale factor as follows:

$$g = Z_{j}^{H} \left[\frac{1}{\sum_{i-1}^{n} \left(\frac{E_{i,t}}{Y_{ij}} \right)} \right] \text{ for } \frac{N_{j,t}^{H}}{N_{j,t}^{H*}} > Z_{j}^{H}$$

and

$$g = \frac{N_{j,t}^{H*}}{A_{j,t}^{H*}} \left[\frac{1}{\sum\limits_{i=1}^{n} \dfrac{E_{i,t}}{Y_{ij}}} \right] \text{ for } N_j^{H*} < N_j^{HS}$$

Otherwise g is determined by equation (11) so as to make the sum of the tract populations equal the total population estimate.

Finally, we must calculate the distribution of household categories l within the total number of households in a particular census tract. We know that the distribution of household types within a community is partially determined by propensities of different household types to travel different distances to work. Also, households tend to cluster around other households of the same type.

$$\begin{pmatrix} \text{reallocated} \\ \text{households,} \\ \text{type } l \end{pmatrix} = \mathscr{F} \left[\begin{pmatrix} \text{households, type } l \\ \text{already at } j \end{pmatrix} + \begin{pmatrix} \text{willingness to} \\ \text{travel to work} \\ \text{of type } l \text{ house-} \\ \text{holds} \end{pmatrix} \right]$$

$$N_{j,t}^{H1} = r_j \left(p_1 N_{j,t-1}^{H1*} + w_1 \sum_{i=1}^{n} \left[\frac{E_{i,t}}{Y_{ij}} \right] \right) \tag{14}$$

where r_j is such that:

$$\sum_{1=1}^{n} N_{j,t}^{H1} = N_{j,t}^{H} \quad \text{and} \tag{15}$$

$$N_{j,t}^{H1*} = N_{j,t}^{H1} + N_{j,t-1}^{H1*} \tag{16}$$

Notation:
$A =$ Area of land (1,000 square feet)
$E =$ Employment (number of persons)
$N =$ Population (number of households)
$Y =$ Index of trip distribution (access parameter)
$Z =$ Constraints.
The following superscripts and subscripts are used:

$U =$ Unusable (land) – given or forecasted

B = Exogenous sector (activity levels not determined by regional economic activities – given or forecasted

R = Retail and service sector

H = Household sector

P = Public and semi-public land use – given or forecasted

S = 'Stable' land (or households and establishments) considered unallocable during time period since the previous land use allocation. 'Total land' less 'Stable land' defines land available for reallocation during the analysis time period.

k = Categories of establishments within retail and service sector

m = Number of such categories

l = Categories of households within residential sector

h = Number of such categories

i, j = Individual census tracts

n = Number of such tracts

t = Time of present land use analysis

T = Time of 'final' land use analysis

$a, b, c, d, e, f, g, r, p, w,$ = unspecified functions

$*$ = Total for areal unit specified.

3.7. PROJECTIVE LAND USE MODEL – PLUM: THEORY AND APPLICATION (VOL. 2)

William Goldner, Stephen R. Rosenthal and Jack R. Meredith

Institute of Transportation and Traffic Engineering,
University of California, Berkeley, Calif.
March 1972

PLUM-IP (Incremental process), 1971

The PLUM model continues to grow, and the version described in this report differs from the earlier version in at least three major points:

a. Comparative statics is no longer used. Instead, increments to all input variables such as population are allocated by the modelling process, adding one or more 'layers' of growth to the base year state of the region. Empirically this was found to improve the model's performance significantly.

b. Allocation to residential zones no longer depends only on a time-distance function. Zone-specific residential attractiveness characteristics and associated development constraints have been added, as suggested by Wilson.

c. A set of supplementary models has been appended to PLUM providing capabilities for predicting household income levels and various tax revenue potentials.

Allocation

The manner by which residential housing and local-serving activities are generated from zonal 'basic' employment is termed the 'allocation' process. Conceptually, the allocation process combines accessibility, opportunities or holding capacity, relative attractiveness, and infrastructure constraints. The heart of this process consists of three allocation matrices which simulate: (1) the journey from workplace to residence; (2) the trip between workplaces and business-serving establishments; and (3) the trip between residences and people-serving establishments.

These matrices are generated from two basic sets of data: travel time tables and 'attractor' information. The travel time data indicates, via a distance-decay function, the inclination of workers and shoppers to commute from one place to another. Free-flow times are used except in the case of the journey between workplace and residence where the peak-flow time is deemed more appropriate.

The attractors vary with the journey of interest. For the workplace-to-the-residence trip the attractor is the number of 'opportunities' for new residential development. For both business- and people-serving establishments, the base-year configurations of local-serving employment are used as attractors.

The time-distance function

The location of worker's residences and local-serving establishments about the respective centers they serve is represented in PLUM as a 'volcano-shaped' distribution which is then modified by the attractors. Cross-sectionally it appears to be a skewed-normal distribution spun concentrically about the origin. This representation follows from the consideration of zoning ordinances and the propensity of people to trade off commuting cost (and profits) for rent. The specific probability of a worker at place of origin being allocated to a unit at the zone of destination is the concept to be modeled.

A density function which meets these requirements is the reciprocal transformation in logarithmic form, adjusted to accommodate to the condition that unit area constitutes the destination:

$$\frac{dp}{dt} = \frac{\beta}{t^3} e^{(\alpha - \beta/t)} = \frac{1}{t}\left[\frac{\beta}{t^2} e^{(\alpha - \beta/t)}\right]$$

For allocations along a line, the function in the brackets is appropriate. However, allocations to annular rings around the origin encounter areas that increase proportionally with the time-distance measure t, and for unit area, the allocation probability is thus divided by t. Because these probabilities are later normalized, it is not necessary to insure that the probabilities are exhaustive at this point.

Advantages of this function are:

a. It has the appropriate skewed-normal shape.
b. As time-distance $t \to 0$, $dp/dt \to 0$.
c. As $t \to \infty$, $dp/dt \to 0$.
d. The mode occurs at $\beta/3$ and hence may be calibrated from actual data.
e. A second parameter in the function exists, α, by which a finite time-distance limit to the laborshed may be imposed.

In PLUM a maximum commute time of 90 minutes is assumed. Integrating the density function out to $t = 90$ and normalizing this to 1.0 (because everyone is assumed to find shelter somewhere), results in a value of $\alpha = \beta/90$.

In lieu of using actual travel times and actual employment and residential locations, PLUM uses virtual times and locations in the form of zonal centroids. Minimum peak- and free-flow times among these centroids, referred to as the 'skim tree', provide the travel time values, t, for use in the density function above.

The probability of workplaces and residences being allocated to a specific zonal centroid is determined within the computer by dividing the parameter t into 3-minute intervals and computing the probability of lying in that interval from the density function (with α and β calibrated from base year data). If no centroid lies in some particular interval then the accumulated workplaces and residences are carried over to the next interval.

The attractor modification

After obtaining the matrix $P = [p(i, j)]$, from the time-distance density function where $p(i, j)$ represents, for example, the probability of a worker in zone i residing in zone j, the attractor information is then used to amplify each probability (to unit area) by the number of opportunities in each zone of destination. The attractors, $O(j)$, disaggregated by zone, are multiplied by $p(i, j)$ to weight each zone by its attractiveness and the products are then normalized by the row sum of the weights, $\sum_i p(i,j) O(j)$ to return the array to the form of a probability matrix.

The residential attractor

For the residential attractor, the number of 'opportunities' for new residential development in zone i, $O(i)$, depends upon both the availability of new residential land and the constraints upon the development of this land within the planning period. Land availability is expressed as the residential holding capacity of the zone; i.e. the product of the vacant residential acreage in the zone, $a_v(i)$, and the average number of housing units per residential acre in that zone, $h(i)/a_r(i)$.[1] Opportunities extend the existing density in the zone to the available residential land.

The land development constraint is an approximation to the area in the zone served by adequate infrastructure, if it were known. Zones may have large quantities of vacant land but are still not developable due to the time-lag in supplying infrastructure. Utilities, water sewers, schools, local government services, and other elements of the infrastructure cannot be supplied instantly; it takes years, sometimes decades, for all these elements to be emplaced. For zones with relatively little development the constraint (expressed as a proportion between zero and one) should be predominant, but for zones almost totally developed, the constraint should have virtually no effect.

A function with this property is:

$$G(x) = \frac{1 - e^{-3x}}{1 - e^{-3}}$$

1. In PLUM vacant land is subdivided into two categories: 'industrial' vacant (i.e. basic plus local-serving) and 'other' vacant (i.e. residential).

where x is the fraction of usable land developed. This function is invoked when zones have little development but quickly increases so that it has a negligible effect with moderate increases in development. For example, at zero percent development the constraint is fully binding whereas at ten percent development the constraint is almost half gone.

The usual application of $G(x)$ is in the form of an upper limit threshold, although one has the choice of emplacing the concept within the allocation function. In the latter case, the number of opportunities is computed as:

$$O(j) = a_v(j) \left[h(j)/a_r(j) \right] G[x(j)]$$

for each zone (j).

Local-serving derivation and allocation

The local-serving sector is derived from a variant of the economic base multiplier concept. Local-serving employment is related to basic population (and thus basic potential demand for local goods and services) rather than basic employment. The difference is two-fold: (1) With population generating the demand, a separation can be made between residential demand and firm demand. (2) PLUM generates local-serving employment in spatially disaggregated form; thus the residential preferences of basic employees, the spatial characteristics of family size, and the zonal differences in the propensity to commute all have an important impact on the distribution of local-serving employment.

The 'attractiveness' factor for local-serving firms is the base year local-serving zonal employment. This has the tendency to emplace the increment in local-serving employment over the base year in the same location as previous local-serving establishments and thus constitutes a natural, built-in inertia to maintain and reinforce existing local-serving centers. In addition, this procedure helps to include the environmental factors of firm location that Alonso (1964) and Wingo (1961) point out accessibility, competition, enhancing elements, and time-cost tradeoff preferences of the local customer

Land use

The next phase of the model allocates land by use. Predicted increments in employment and residences are reconciled by zone with the availability of land, recognizing the tendency for commercial uses to displace residential uses. Reflecting such economic priorities, land is allocated within PLUM in the following order: unusable, basic, local-serving, residential, vacant.

Although the allocation functions generate the spatial distributions of workers to their residential locations, there is still the problem of transforming these allocations from workers to housing units. The spatial demand for housing units and the acreage upon which they are located closely follows contemporary rent and land value theory . . . . However instead of land prices being associated with parcel size, the zone-specific average residential density is used as a surrogate. Thus land occupancy is a function of density, subject to the condition that each worker is insured a place of residence. Densities can be changed systematically, either as a policy-generated adjustment, or in response to the degree of development pressure in the zone.

The calculation sequence

. . . PLUM is currently run as an incremental model; it projects a growth increment for the time period between the base year and the target year. Then it adds the increment to the existing base inventories to arrive at a projected *level* for the target year. More specifically, the calculation sequence in PLUM is as follows:

1. Basic employment at place of work is allocated to a place of residence. Each worker allocated becomes a member of a zonal pool which is formed into households by a zone-specific worker per household ratio.
2. Basic workers at place of work and basic population at place of residence generate demands for services thus determining local-serving employment at place of work and local-serving land absorption.
3. Total employment (basic plus local-serving) is allocated to a place of residence and a family size associated with each worker as in 1.
4. Housing units and residential land absorption are calculated.
5. Land is then allocated for 'highest and best' use in the order of (1) land unusable or reserved for open space (policy-determined open space), (2) basic (including unique locators), (3) local-serving, (4) residential, and (5) the residual, if any. Over-allocations are handled by either increasing densities (as in a downtown area) or reallocating activities to zones with vacant land.
6. These allocations are performed for growth increments between the base and target years. Employment, population, and land activity projections made for the target years are derived by adding the projected increments to the base year levels.

Definition of variables

The following list of variables is used in the PLUM equation system. The variables are collected here with their definitions as a reference aid in understanding the mathematical equations in the rest of this chapter.

Capital letters represent allocation functions, key ratios, multipliers, correction factors:

$P_{wh}(i, j)$	= work-to-home allocation probability function
$P_{hl}(i, j)$	= home-to-local-serving-business allocation probability function
$P_{wl}(i, j)$	= work-to-local-serving-business allocation probability function
$\dot{K}$	= multiplier (for incremental values)
$\hat{L}(i)$	= population per employed resident (for the base year)
$L'(i)$	= population per employed resident (after adding the growth increment)
$\hat{H}(i)$	= population per housing unit (for the base year)
$H'(i)$	= population per housing unit (after adding the growth increment)
$F'(i)$	= employed residents per housing unit (after) accounting for the increment of population)
$\hat{A}_l(i)$	= land absorption coefficient (base year) for local-serving businesses (acres/employee)
$\hat{A}_r(i)$	= land absorption coefficient (base year) for residences (acres/housing unit; net lot size)
R	= parameter for controlling target year regional housing level
$\dot{C}_1$	= correction to incremental local-serving employment
$\dot{C}_2$	= correction to incremental non-working population
$\dot{C}_3$	= correction to incremental number of housing units
$\dot{C}_4$	= second correction to incremental number of housing units
$\dot{C}_5$	= third correction to incremental number of housing units

$\dot{C}_6$	= correction to incremental employment at place of residence
$\dot{C}_7$	= second correction to incremental non-working population

Small letters represent zonal values of various variables:

$a(i)$	= acreage
$d(i)$	= potential demand for local-serving employment generated from within a zone.
$e(i)$	= employment at place of work; number of jobs
$h(i)$	= number of housing units
$n(i)$	= residential population
$q(i)$	= residential non-working population
$r(i)$	= residential working population; employed residents
$x(i), y(i)$	= intermediate functions used in the constraint phase

Single subscripts denote activities or land uses and apply to vectors:

z_b	= connected with basic employment
z_e	= connected with employment
z_k	= vacant land reserved for local-serving and basic industries (industrial vacant)
z_l	= connected with local-serving employment
z_r	= connected with residences
z_s	= connected with streets/highways
z_t	= total: sum of the components
z_u	= unusable
z_v	= vacant (other)
z_w	= connected with workplace

Superscripts are used to denote other attributes of a variable:

$\hat{z}$	= base year stock
$\dot{z}$	= incremental stock
$z', z'', z''', z^{iv}, z^{v}, z^{vi}$	= successively calculated values
$\tilde{z}$	= intermediate stock
z^*	= final output stock

Phase 1: Allocation

The increment to basic employment is distributed from place of work j to place of residence i, by a work-to-home allocation probability function which is constructed in several stages. Basically, this allocation function is a composite of two types of variables: travel-time network and 'opportunities.'

The travel-time portion defines the probability $P_{wh}^*(i,j)$ 'per opportunity' in zone i, that an employee working in zone j will want to live at the distance of zone i. This distance is represented by the skim tree times, $t(i,j)$, grouped into three-minute intervals between these zones;

$$P_{wh}^*(i, j) = \left(\frac{1}{t(i, j)}\right)* \left\{ exp[\beta/90 - \beta/t(i, j)] \right.$$
$$\left. - exp[\beta/90 - \beta(t(i, j) - 3)] \right\}, \tag{1}$$

which is what is actually calculated in running the computer program. The allocation is to only those zones for which $t(i,j) < 90$; i.e. for $t(i,j) \geq 90$, $P_{wh}^*(i, j) = 0$.

The number of 'opportunities', $O_h(i)$, for new residential development in zone (i) depends upon the holding capacity of vacant land.

$$O_h(i) = \frac{\hat{a}_v(i) * \hat{h}(i)}{\hat{a}_r(i)} \tag{2}$$

This equation has been deleted from this part of the model   (3)

The composite work-to-home allocation probability function is then constructed as a normalized product of the travel time distribution and the 'opportunities':

$$P_{wh}(i,j) = \frac{P_{wh}^*(i,j) * O_h(i)}{\sum_i P_{wh}^*(i,j) * O_h(i)} \tag{4}$$

Finally, the increment to basic employment is distributed from the place of work (j) to place of residence (i) by the use of this probability function:

$$\dot{r}_b(i) = \sum_j P_{wh}(i, j) * \dot{e}_b(j) \tag{5}$$

Values of the ratio of population per employed resident for each zone are calculated from base year values of total residential population and total working population at place of residence:

$$\hat{L}(i) = \frac{\hat{n}_t(i)}{\hat{r}t(i)} \tag{6}$$

The increment to residential non-working population in basic employees' households is calculated from the above values of basic employees at place of residence and population per employed resident;

$$\dot{q}'_b(i) = \left[\hat{L}(i) - 1\right] * \dot{r}'_b(i) \tag{7}$$

The multiplier is computed as the ratio of the total increment of local-serving employment (an input) to the total increment of population connected with basic employment:

$$\dot{K} = \frac{\sum_i \dot{e}_l(i)}{\sum_i \dot{e}_b(i) + \sum_i \dot{q}'_b(i)} \tag{8}$$

The potential demand at place of residence, $d_{rb}(i)$, for local-serving (l/s) employment servicing residential non-working population in basic employee's households in zone (i) is calculated by applying the multiplier to the incremental value calculated in (7):

$$\dot{d}_{rb}(i) = \dot{K} * \dot{q}'_b(i) \tag{9}$$

Similarly, the potential demand for l/s employment serving basic industry and its employees is calculated by applying the multiplier to the increment of basic employment:

$$\dot{d}_{eb}(i) = \dot{K} * \dot{e}_b(i) \tag{10}$$

The increment $\dot{e}_{hl}(i)$ to local-serving employment serving residences is calculated for each zone from the demand calculated in (9), by applying the home-to-local-serving-business allocation probability function:

$$\dot{e}_{hl}(i) = \sum_j P_{hl}(i,j) * \dot{d}'_{rb}(j) \tag{11}$$

Note that $\sum_i \dot{e}'_{hl}(i) = \sum_i \dot{d}'_{rb}(i)$

Similarly, the increment $\dot{e}'_{wl}(i)$ to local-serving employment serving workplaces is calculated for each zone from the demand calculated in (10) by applying the work-to-local-serving-business allocation probability function:

$$\dot{e}'_{wl}(i) = \sum_j P_{wl}(i, j) * \dot{d}'_{eb}(j) \tag{12}$$

Here also $\sum_i \dot{e}_{wl}(i) = \sum_i \dot{d}_{eb}(i)$.

The increment of local-serving employment is the sum of the two parts calculated above:

$$\dot{e}'_l(i) = \dot{e}'_{hl}(i) + \dot{e}'_{wl}(i) \tag{13}$$

A correction factor, C_1, is calculated to neutralize the computational rounding errors that may result from the successive application of K, P_{hl} and P_{wl} in equations (8)–(12).

$$\dot{C}_1 = \frac{\sum_i \dot{e}_l(i)}{\sum_i \dot{e}'_l(i)} \tag{14}$$

where $\sum_l \dot{e}_l(i)$ is the area-wide total of l/s employment change. The correction factor is applied to the incremental local-serving employment:

$$\dot{e}''_l(i) = \dot{C}_1 * \dot{e}'_l(i) \tag{15}$$

Thus, $\sum_i \dot{e}''_l(i) = \sum_i \dot{e}_l(i)$.

The increment to total employment at place of work for each zone is the sum of input incremental basic employment and calculated incremental local-serving employment:

$$\dot{e}'_l(i) = \dot{e}_b(i) + \dot{e}''_l(i) \tag{16}$$

This incremental employment at place of work is now distributed to residences in accordance with the work-to-home allocation probability function:

$$\dot{r}_t'(i) = \sum_j P_{wh}(i, j) * \dot{e}_t(j) \tag{17}$$

The increment to total residential non-working population is calculated from the above value of incremental total employment at place of residence and the ratio [from (6)] of population per employed resident:

$$\dot{q}_t''(i) = [\hat{L}(i) - 1] * \dot{r}_t'(i) \tag{18}$$

Since this equation applies a base year value $\hat{L}$ to incremental variables, a correction factor must be applied:

$$C_2 = \frac{\sum\limits_i \dot{q}_t(i)}{\sum\limits_i q_t''(i)} \tag{19}$$

where $\sum_i \dot{q}_t(i)$ is the area-wide total of residential non-working population.

$$q_t'''(i) = C_2 * q_t''(i), \text{ so that } \sum_i \dot{q}_t'''(i) = \sum_i \dot{q}_t(i) \tag{20}$$

Now the total increment to residential population for each zone can be calculated as the sum of working and non-working population at place of residence:

$$\dot{n}_t'(i) = \dot{r}_t'(i) + q_t'''(i) \tag{21}$$

Comments on calibration

Calibration involves 'fine tuning' a model to most adequately reflect a particular application of interest. Models should be re-calibrated when they are applied to new geographic areas or, periodically, for areas where new data sources are available. Calibration in short, is a process of experimentation aimed at determining the sensitivity of a model to changes in its parameters and, thereby, evaluating the design of the model's components. The calibration process is complete when particular values for each parameter have been established and the model is ready for use as a 'production tool.' For PLUM, calibration involves a special sequence of model projections over some historical period, (i.e. the 'target' year has already occurred). In addition to the usual modes of analyzing the PLUM projections, calibration runs offer the opportunity to compare some key PLUM forecasts with actual historical observations.

The *ideal* calibration process results in a model (with associated parameters) which is 'accurate'. Operationally, this means that one can demonstrate that the model 'works', by using it to simulate (i.e. recreate) the experience of some historical test period. In *practice*, calibration is often an elusive process, more an art than a science. In an attempt to provide a sound understanding of the calibration process, some of the major considerations in calibrating PLUM are identified and some fundamental guidelines are presented in the following paragraphs.

PLUM calibration can be viewed as a special case of the general problem of output evaluation.

Data problems

Data limitations often force the calibration process to be less than ideal. More specifically, if a calibration is being performed from a 'base' period to some 'target' period (both prior to the present data), it is often difficult to acquire complete, accurate and consistent data profiles for these two periods. Almost inevitably, the data used for calibration have varying degrees of reliability, reflecting differing sources, different methods of reporting and collection, non-comparable definitions and dates, and wide variations in errors of measurement. (Even successive censuses have inaccuracies or do not reflect the same influences.)

To the extent that one lacks complete faith in these 'before and after' data profiles, one should not expect that a model will accurately predict a growth increment in a calibration exercise. Obviously, a model cannot be expected to be aware of exogenous data deficiencies and to automatically adjust for them.

Calibration time period

Even if there were no major uncertainties with the data, the calibration time period can confound the legitimacy of the evaluation process. Suppose that a calibration is attempted over a five-year historical period (e.g. 1965–1970). And assume the growth increment projected by the model for that period differs from that which actually occurred. Is it then erroneous to use that unadjusted model to predict growth of the same metropolitan area for some longer future time interval (e.g. 1970–1990)? Not necessarily.

It is possible that the model in question is quite accurate for the purpose of long-term forecasting (1970–1990) but the dynamic phenomena that it simulates cannot be observed in a very short period (like 1965–1970). Moreover, the short historical period might be dominated by identifiable 'special' situations which one would not expect to continue to influence growth patterns throughout the future long-term planning period. Typical complicating (and confounding) factors that could distort short-run statistics are: time lags between development decisions and completion of construction; 'lumpiness' of development in which statistics suddenly jump due to official completion of a major development project; or unique pilot development projects which are unsuccessful and, in retrospect, are recognized as errors in judgment.[2] For all these reasons, a smoothed process of development inertia is not likely to be observable at a detailed Zonal level within any five-year test period.

Still another argument against the short-run calibration period is that fundamental changes taking place in labor force participation and in the number of workers per household have not had a chance to stabilize statistically in a short period.

Clearly, in the face of such short-term distortions, it would be incorrect to consider the modification of the model's parameters to fit the short-term historical data to be a prerequisite to using it as a long-term forecasting tool. One has to wait for long-term events to be realized and trends to become apparent in order to calibrate truly a long-term model.

Policy implications

Another calibration issue is the extent to which the model remains neutral with regard to specific planning policies and constraints such as zoning regulations or transportation facilities. If a model is calibrated so that it closely reproduces development patterns over a particular historical period, then to some extent it implicitly reflects the key planning policies and constraints that were in effect during that period. To what extent *should* this calibrated model with its associated historical policies be used to create future development projections? In some situations, it might be appropriate to continue to reflect such historical policies. In other

2. For example, PLUM'S conceptual incremental approach is to emplace a layer of development constrained by land availability on top of the historically located activities which reflect the changing and perhaps irrational effects of past locating activity. Because development is 'lumpy' and reflects substantial uncertainty when originally emplaced, the regularities of the development process only begin to smooth out over a fairly long period of time as individual tests of the market are affirmed or found to be in error.

cases these historical policies should be 'updated' for use in future projections or perhaps it would be even more realistic to replace historical
planning constraints or policies with entirely new concepts that are more
relevant for the future. Considering these various basic alternatives, it
is clear that policy assumptions and constraints may force the calibration
attempts to be highly judgmental even if data and measurement errors
are relatively small.

Considering these type of practical issues, the objective of the calibration
process ultimately becomes vague and unscientific. Granted, the model
should be run over some historical test period for which exogenous data
already exist. But having done this, the analyst is faced with a comparison
of two (historical) growth patterns – those derived by the model and that
implied by the most reliable exogenous data. These two patterns should be
similar but not necessarily exact. And if they are different it is often
difficult to say which one is a proper criterion basis for preparing to develop
long-term projections.

If the model appears to have captured the 'essential aspects' of the actual
growth pattern (as approximated by the exogenous data) then one has a
model which is said to be 'calibrated'. If not, one makes 'reasonable'
adjustments to the variable parameters in the model until the model's
'predictions' are more acceptable. But in no event should one blatantly
tamper with a well-motivated model to force it to fit what is essentially a
questionable calibration test. In general, then, calibration can be a time-
consuming, tedious process that is worth serious effort only to the extent
that available data provide a meaningful test of the model's predictive
powers. With this viewpoint in mind, the planner can proceed to calibrate
PLUM . . .

3.8. JOBS, PEOPLE AND LAND (BASS)

CREUE (1968)

Center for Real Estate and Urban Economics,
Institute of Urban and Regional Development,
University of California, Berkeley

Simulation in phases (BASS)

The allocation procedures in the BASS Model may be viewed as a step
further in the direction of an explicit replication of the market process. In

the residential allocation phase, with which we are concerned here, the change in the number of housing units between the start of an iteration, and its completion is seen as a complex of developments which includes (1) the removal of a sizable number of units from the stock due to demolitions, (2) changing the relative values of much of the stock, (3) separating total demand for new housing into subgroups of households with similar housing preferences, (4) partitioning of the land available for housing development into land supplies for the housing types desired by each subgroup, and (5) allocating of demand to supply for each of the housing types.

Breaking down the complexity of the real estate market into subprocesses, as in the BASS Model, has obvious advantages. It offers a greater potential accuracy due to its ability to separate the effects of a variable on one element of the market process from its effect on another. The simulation process also offers the opportunity to pinpoint errors. Its greatest advantage, however, lies in its capacity for giving insight into the market process. To the extent that it simulates the market process, it provides an invaluable laboratory for the testing of various assumptions – assumptions of various relationships within the market process and assumptions of various public policies which affect the market.

Forecasting residential allocation with a simulation model also has some disadvantages. In contrast with the approaches discussed earlier, which need only historical data on a few variables to calibrate the model, the simulation approach requires data for every subprocess that is singled out as a step in the total process. The fact that the output of the model is the result of a multistage process may result in the accumulation of error.[1] The most interesting handicap from a theoretical viewpoint, however, is the assumption inherent in some models (such as BASS) that the market process can be simulated in stages, rather than in the simultaneous solution of the relationships involved. In other words, the market process is a complex whole; the separation of simultaneously interrelated occurrences into a series of occurrences distorts the nature of the market process. . . .

The most important task assigned to the BASS Residential Submodel is the spatial allocating of new housing. In each iteration the model must identify six separate new housing markets (single-family high, middle and low, and multiple-family high, middle and low) each with its own supply, demand and accessibility elements. For example, a portion of the vacant

1. See William Alonso, 'The Quality of Data and the Choice and Design of Predictive Models,' Working Paper No. 72; Berkeley. University of California, Center for Planning and Development Research, 1968.

and agricultural land in each subarea is projected to be potentially developable for middle-value single-family housing units. The number of jobholders working in each subarea and, either because they have a new job or because they desire different accommodations, seeking new middle-value single-family housing from which their job location will be accessible, is estimated. The accessibility or closeness of the supply (the land) in each subarea to the demand (the families seeking housing) is measured, and on the basis of these measurements the families are allocated in varying proportions to the various subareas. These calculations are performed for each of the six housing types. In each new time period the process is repeated for all six housing types, including the recalculation of all supplies, demands and accessibilities.

Demolition and filtering

Demolitions affect both the supply and the demand for new homes. They influence demand by the need for replacements and increase the supply of land available for development. Filtering has been defined as change in the value of housing units relative to the total housing stock.[2] The sale of an older house by a family purchasing a more expensive home to a family with less financial resources is an illustration of filtering.

Forecasts of demolition and filtration calculated for each tract from general equations are not very accurate because very little data suitable for the analysis of these processes is available on a tract level. Forecasts on a regional level, however, are more suitable for analysis primarily because data on regional demolition and filtration rates for housing units of various types are available from the U.S. census.[3] Therefore, in the BASS Residential Submodel, judgmentally constructed equations are used to forecast reasonable relative rates for each tract. These rates are then adjusted so that the regional totals derived from these rates are consistent with the regional rates supplied as input parameters.

To forecast demolitions, the BASS Model utilizes exogenous forecasts of (1) the total demolition rate to constrain the entire demolition process and (2) relative demolition rates for the six housing types subject to the overall

2. For a discussion of filtering, see William Grigsby, *Housing Markets and Public Policy*, Philadelphia, University of Pennsylvania Press, 1963; also, Wallace Smith, *Filtering and Neighborhood Change*, Research Report No. 24, Berkeley, University of California, Center for Real Estate and Urban Economics, 1964.
3. U.S. Bureau of the Census, *U.S. Census of Housing: 1960*, vol. 4, *Components of Inventory Change*, Washington, D.C., Government Printing Office, 1962.

demolition constraint. In brief, the overall demolition parameter determines the total number of demolitions, the relative demolition parameters for the six housing types are used in calculations partitioning the total among the housing types, and the demolitions for each housing type are allocated to the various tracts on the basis of judgmental equations. . . .

The framework for the filtering process in the BASS Residential Submodel is the definitional assumption that a constant proportion of the families in the total region will occupy homes of different value classes in any time period. The proportions 20-40-40 percent for high, middle and low value classes respectively are currently used in the model. . . .

The BASS Model assumes that the total housing stock would always be partitioned into three value classes of constant proportions. The value classes of new units are estimated exogenously and supplied to the model as a parameter. It is clear that following demolitions, filtering, and the addition of new units the proportions will probably shift from their specified shares. If the shift is radical, it is an indication that our fixed parameters are inconsistent. Small deviations, however, can be visualized as the natural adjustment of the market to gradually changing quantities of demand and supply. This simulates the real world situation where the new housing built primarily for the high and middle-income families can hasten the filtering of older housing to low-income families and, conversely, a greater willingness to let older housing be occupied by lower-income families at a low price elicits a higher production level for new houses.

The model implements this trade-off by forcing the estimates of new production and filtering for each housing type to adjust in proportion to the number of units in its category. Because existing housing is more numerous than new, this procedure, as intended, forces greater adjustments in the filtration process than in the projected cost distribution of new construction.

The accuracy of this demolition and filtering submodel is limited, primarily by the lack of information concerning the factors involved in demolition and filtering. However, its forecasts appear to be reasonable. The development of markedly improved simulations of this process will require significantly better data. . . .

Potential supply of new housing units

The potential supply of new housing units for a tract is assumed to be dependent on six factors: (1) slope of the land, (2) attractiveness of the tract for residential development, (3) the value class distribution of housing units, (4) the proportion of single-family and multi-family dwellings, (5) the density of development, and (6) the potential land supply for new housing units.

The slope of the usable land in each tract is graded as level, rolling or hilly. The BASS general guidelines classified land with a predominant slope of less than 5 percent as level, 5 to 15 percent as rolling, and up to 30 percent as hilly. Attractiveness includes factors such as competition from other potential uses, climate, and the lack of amenity due to industrial plants in the tract. The value class distribution of existing households and the relative percentages of single-family and multi-family units are self-explanatory. The density of development is defined as the sum of population and employment in the tract divided by the total usable land in the tract whether it is presently in use or not. The value of this variable for tract j is calculated by averaging the density of the four closest tracts (including tract j), each weighted with the inverse of the time distance squared.

$$DD_j = \frac{\sum_{i=1}^{4} DDT_i / TD_{ij}^2}{\sum_{i=1}^{4} 1/TD_{ij}^2}$$

where

DD_j = adjusted density of development of tract j
DDT_i = initial density of development of tract i
TD_{ij} = travel time between tract i and tract j.

This 'smoothing' is done for two reasons: (1) the effects of historical factors no longer relevant are mitigated, and (2) the effect of increasing urbanization in nearby tracts is transmitted to tract j in a manner akin to the 'domino theory'.[4]

---

4. The price of land is neither an input to nor an output from the BASS Model as it is the intermediate point of the market process rather than the initiating factor or the resulting outcome. Other researchers have found that land prices are highly correlated with the density of development; see Robert Schmitt, 'Population Densities and Real Property Values in a Metropolitan Area, *Land Economics*, November 1959.

Partitioning of the potential supply of new housing units

The BASS Residential Submodel attempts to partition the supply of potential housing in each tract roughly in proportion to the expected development of units for each of the six housing types.

The partitioning of the potential supply into single-family and multi-family units is based on the average of two ratios. The first is the ratio of existing single-family and multi-family units in each tract. The second, which is weighted twice as heavily, is the ratio of potential single-family and multi-family units calculated as a function of the density of development in each tract. The algorithm used is as follows:[5]

$$\text{for } DD_j < 5 \; PSF_j = 1.18 - 0.30 \cdot DD_j^{1/4}$$

$$\text{for } DD_j > 5 \; PSF_j = 1.48 - 0.50 \cdot DD_j^{1/4}$$

where

PSF_j = not less than 0.
PSF_j = is the percentage of single-family dwellings projected in tract j
DD_j = is the existing density of development in tract j.

The two ratios for each tract are averaged to reflect the compromise between the economic forces which may be making change feasible and the efforts of neighborhoods to resist change.

The potential supply of new single-family and multi-family housing units in each tract is then partitioned into high, medium and low housing value classes. This is estimated in the BASS Model by averaging three sets of proportions: (1) the proportion of existing housing by value class, (2) the proportion of potential housing by value class based on the density of development, and (3) the proportion of potential units by value class based on the slope of the land. The first proportion is the existing value distribution of housing in the tract and surrounding tracts. For the second proportion a percentage of units equal to the numerical value of the density of development are shifted from the potential low-value group. If the density is greater than 100 all low value units are shifted. For the third

---

5. The equation used to calculate PSF and the equations used to partition by value class were derived from the analysis of the patterns of development in approximately thirty communities in the region. The same data provided the basis for the residential land use coefficients.

proportion, if the slope is hilly all of the potential low-value units in the supply are shifted to potential high-value units, while rolling land results in a shift of one-half of the low-value units, and no shift takes place if the land is classified as level.

The three proportions are averaged with equal weight. Although research could probably add some elegance to this procedure, it was not given high priority because data of the quality needed to isolate the effects of existing development, the density of development, and slope of terrain are not presently available. . . .

Potential land supply for new housing units

The basic data input used in forecasting the supply of new housing units is the quantity of land available for development, which includes all agricultural acreage, most vacant land, and land freed as a result of employment migration or housing demolition. The inclusion of agricultural land assumes that urban land use will continue to outbid agricultural use if more urban land is needed. Vacant land was excluded when development was unlikely due to its physical nature, such as steeply sloping (over 30 percent), and marshy or underwater land. The future addition of an algorithm to gradually shift this unusable land into the usable category as the demand for developable land increased in that tract would increase the sophistication of the model in long-range forecasting.

The BASS Model currently makes no provision for competing land uses (e.g. residential and industrial) to bid against each other for the land. In a tract where such competition was likely to occur or where other factors made residential development less attractive (e.g. inferior soil conditions or harsh climate), a flag was inserted which limited land available for residential development to an estimated percentage of the total developable land for that tract. In the current runs these flags were utilized only in the more obvious situations. A careful consideration of their more extensive use would appear warranted in refining the accuracy of the model. The danger should be noted, however, that adjusting development in many tracts to 'expected' levels substitutes the modeler's judgment for the model's power of prediction.

Determination of total potential supply of new housing units

The calculation of total potential supply of new housing units for each tract is determined by the amount of land absorbed by residential units of various types, as shown in the following equation.

$$TPS_j = \frac{LAND_j}{\sum_{i=1,6} PNH_j^i \cdot LAC_j^i}$$

where

TPS_j = total potential supply of new housing units in tract j
$LAND_j$ = potential land supply in tract j
PNH_j^i = percentage of potential new housing of type i in tract j
LAC_j^i = land absorption coefficient for new housing units of type i for tract j. . . .

Following the determination of the potential supply of new housing units for each tract, the land absorption coefficients are held in reserve until the conclusion of the allocation of residential development among the potential supply. They are then used to update the land stock vectors, adding land absorbed by new residential development in each tract to the residential land vector and removing it from the vacant land category.

Demand for new housing

The total demand for new housing for the region is expressed as the sum of housing units removed from the stock (demolition) and the new families projected by the exogenous regional growth model described in chapter 2. The total demand is first partitioned into single-family and multi-family units. . . .

The total demand, after being divided into single-family and multi-family units is then partitioned into the three value classes. The partitions of the housing units built from 1950 to 1960 between high, middle and low value classes were 36, 52, and 12 percent for single-family, and 19, 51, and 30 percent for multi-family. Many experts predict that the expected continued prosperity in the United States will tend to make it possible for a larger proportion of families on the lower half of the income scale to participate in the new-home market. On the other hand, as the Bay Area develops, new units will represent a smaller fraction of the total. A greater proportion of the market will accommodate families filtering up with a smaller percentage built primarily to accommodate the influx of new families. These factors will tend to balance each other. Thus the initial run of the model was made under the assumption that the relative sizes of the different segments of the population participating in the new-home market, which have been fairly constant for many years, will not change radically. One of the runs under an alternative assumption, . . . postulated increased rates of demolition with a greater proportion of new units built for low-income families to replace demolished units.

Accessibility

At this point the demand for new housing units and the potential supply of new housing units are each expressed for the same six housing categories and only spatial location remains to be considered. In general, the calculation of accessibility, the attribute of spatial location of concern here, raises two questions – Accessible to what? and – How should accessibility be measured?

Accessibility to three types of activity appears to play an important role in the determination of new housing location: (1) accessibility to neighborhood facilities such as schools and shopping centers, (2) accessibility to the urban core and its attractions, and (3) accessibility to employment based on the assumption that most households decide on housing location with the job location of the head of household as the primary spatial constraint. The first, accessibility to neighborhood attractions, may be highly desirable to renters and buyers but is a consideration for microanalysis and of little significance for a metropolitan land development model. Delineating the role of accessibility to the city core for use in the BASS Model would be difficult. First, its value varies markedly among households and second, it is highly correlated with most employment accessibility measures. Therefore, accessibility to employment is the only measure used in determining accessibility. However, the BASS Residential Submodel is now developed to the stage where the search for a more sensitive measure of accessibility – a measure including accessibility to other activities as well as employment – should be considered.

Having for the present runs restricted accessibility to the spatial relationship with respect to employment, the choice of employment variables to be used remains. The ideal (complete knowledge) solution would involve knowing the jobsite (or sites) of jobholders in the specific households seeking new housing. This method is impractical with current tools due to three limitations: (1) data relating household location to job location for the region does not exist; (2) even if the initial inventory were available, we do not know enough about the movement of families to update the inventory in the demolition and filtering phases of the residential allocation process; (3) such a solution would be too expensive to calculate with existing computers.

The BASS Residential Submodel uses an employment variable generated as a weighted average of previously existing employment and employment added during the employment allocation phase of the iteration.

$$\text{PHD}_i = \alpha \cdot \frac{\text{NE}_i}{\sum\limits_j \text{NE}_j} + \beta \cdot \frac{\text{E}_i}{\sum\limits_j \text{E}_j}$$

where

PHD_i = the proportion of total housing demand employed in tract i
NE_i = new employment in tract i
E_i = previously existing employment in tract i
α, β = weighting factors totaling unity.

Compromises can be noticed in this procedure. Employees who are not heads of households are included in the calculations and employees in each tract are assumed to represent the same distribution of household type and to have the same locating characteristics.

This weighted employment variable differentiates between the two basic components of new housing demand; (1) that necessitated by the net incremental employment of the area (NE_i), and (2) that due to families upgrading their housing, which is a function of E_i. Accessibility measured with respect to existing employment alone would result in new housing construction lagging far behind demand in subareas with strong employment growth. In the 1965–1970 iteration of the BASS Model, 38 percent of the new construction was allocated according to the existing employment component and 62 percent associated with accessibility to new employment. As the ratio of new to existing units becomes less in each iteration, the upgrading factor may be expected to become more dominant. Consequently the proportion of demand for new housing keyed to existing employment is increased by 2 percent per iteration.

The remaining question is: How should accessibility be measured? The BASS Residential Submodel utilizes a procedure similar to that proposed in 1959 by Walter Hansen, a transportation engineer studying City Planning at MIT.[6] In general this approach calculates for each tract a variable, termed accessibility, which is a sum of the demand accessible to the tract weighted by a friction factor, a function of time, distance, and/or cost:

$$A_i = \sum_{j=1,NT} PHD_j \cdot F_{ij}$$

A_i = accessibility of tract i
F_{ij} = the friction factor between tracts i and j
NT = the number of tracts.

The proportion of land developed in each tract can then be estimated as a function of the accessibility variable.[7]

The gravity model of the form $1/x^\alpha$ where x is a friction variable and α a parameter has commonly been used to express the distribution of trip lengths. Hansen noted that researchers usually found that journey-to-work trips fitted to this form had an α of about 0.9, social trips an α of about 1.1 and shopping trips an α of 2.0. He thus suggested using the following algorithm to calculate accessibility:

$$A_i = \sum_i \frac{E_i}{D_{ij}^{0.9}}$$

where

j = 1, NT
D_{ij} = the distance between tracts i and j
E_i = employment in tract i.

It is doubtful, however, if the distribution of journey-to-work trips for the occupants of newly constructed housing units exhibits the same pattern as the distribution of journey-to-work trips for households occupying older housing. The BASS Model uses a linear function of estimated commuting time, dropping from unity at the origin to zero at 50 minutes, to calculate

6. Walter G. Hansen, 'How Accessibility Shapes Land Use', *Journal of the American Institute of Planners*, Vol. 25, May 1959, pp. 73–76. For discussions of earlier contributions see: Paul F. Wendt, *The Dynamics of Central City Land Values – San Francisco and Oakland, 1950–1960*, Research Report No. 18, Berkeley. University of California, Center for Real Estate and Urban Economics, 1961; and Walter Isard, ed., *Methods of Regional Analysis: An Introduction to Regional Science*, New York: Wiley and Sons, 1960.
7. Hansen found the equation $DR_i = 13.7 \cdot A^{2.7}$ (where DR_i = ratio of developed to total land in tract i) to best express the relationship for Washington, D.C.

accessibility. However, experimentation with other curves has convinced us that the model is not very sensitive to changes in the function except for extensive shifts, e.g. emphasizing nearby sites markedly over moderate commutes. For example, gravity functions with the parameter α equal to or greater than 2 yield significantly different results.

Many different elements have been suggested as components of the commuting time friction variable measuring hindrance to travel. Distance, time by automobile, time by transit, money cost and the level of service are among them. The imminent presence of the Bay Area Rapid Transit System with fast commute times for specific trips suggests that a straight distance measure would be inaccurate, but experimentation suggested that the model would be insensitive to the inclusion of any of the other possible elements.

The last step in the residential allocation process as simulated in the BASS Model is the assignment of new housing as a function of the accessibility variable. In real estate terminology, it is assumed that developers and builders locate their product in the subareas with the greatest accessibility to locating families subject to an offsetting attraction of outlying areas due to the lower prices on more remote parcels. In the BASS Model, the only differentiation among the housing types in this process is between single-family and multiple housing units. Given the limited data – no satisfactory inventory of housing units by value class exists for two points in time – the value class distinctions cannot be measured. This simplification is discussed more fully later in the context of possible future improvements of the model.

The BASS study initially hypothesized that the percentage of the supply actually developed for housing in each subarea would be proportional to the accessibility raised to an appropriate power, A^{α}. The best fit was obtained using $\alpha = 1.8$ for single-family and 3.0 for multi-family housing units. However, a polynomial regression analysis for the period 1960 to 1965 resulted in multiple correlation coefficients of less than 0.3 for any equation of this form. Additional regression analysis with logarithmic expressions resulted in the following equations which yielded multiple correlation coefficients of 0.7 for single-family and 0.5 for multi-family housing units:

single-family $\text{DP}_j^i = \text{SH}_j^i \cdot 0.07065 \cdot e^{[0.90 \cdot \text{ALOG}(A_j)]}$

multi-family $\text{DP}_j^i = \text{SH}_j^i \cdot 0.445 \cdot e^{[0.44 \cdot \text{ALOG}(A_j)]}$

where

DP_j^i = is proportional to the percentage of supply developed
SH_j^i = supply of housing of type i in tract j
$ALOG(A_j)$ = the antilog of the accessibility for tract j.

The final note concerns a difficulty with the accessibility concept in a region such as the San Francisco Bay Area. The land supply accessible to San Francisco's housing demand has a potential for development incommensurate with its measure of accessibility, because much of the land area surrounding San Francisco is bar or ocean or else is already developed. The limited supply of existing land accessible to the city's employment therefore enjoys a favorable position in the real estate market. Comparison of the San Jose and Sacramento areas again illustrates this problem. Only a limited amount of developable land is available in the valleys near San Jose while Sacramento is almost surrounded by flat plains most of which present no development problems. If we hypothetically posit a similar housing demand originating from employment in each of these two cities, it is clear that two comparable units of supply, one near each city, with equal travel times to the city center will have similar measures of accessibility. Yet it is obvious that the unit of supply near San Jose will have a higher possibility of being developed because, relative to the Sacramento market, it faces considerably less competition.

The only feasible solution for the immediate runs seemed to be an adjustment of all accessibilities in certain portions of the region. For an area like San Joaquin County the tuning was straightforward because the distance of Stockton from other major employment centers results in almost no commuting across the county boundaries. In an area like San Mateo there is extensive commuting and this factor must be taken into account as the accessibilities are adjusted.

4. Miscellaneous other models

4.1. INTRODUCTION

The preceding sections of this book have each focused on a particular model construct and its subsequent variants and elaborations. This section is quite different in that several different models are described. These are, for the most part, unrelated.

The Lathrop-Hamburg model is a macro-descriptive model, which has a somewhat different view of urban spatial processes, different from the Lowry viewpoint presented in the previous section of this book. Both the Lathrop-Hamburg construct, and the Lowry construct can however, be expressed (as discussed earlier for Lowry) in terms of the Wilson entropy maximizing approach.

The next group of excerpts (Chapin and Weiss, Kaiser) represent a small portion of the work done at the Center for Urban and Regional Studies at the Chapel Hill campus of the University of North Caroline (UNC). This work takes a somewhat more micro-level view of residential development, with a particular emphasis on the phenomenon of residential subdivision development at the urban fringe. The work would be properly described as micro-descriptive (or perhaps more accurately as meso-descriptive), and has yielded some rather interesting results which have been underutilized by other workers in the field.

The third group of excerpts (Herbert and Stevens, and Harris) describe a model construct which may also be called micro-descriptive or micro-behavioral. This model, the Herbert-Stevens model, has a somewhat more micro-economic theoretical basis which has recently been shown to relate to a special case of the entropy maximizing formulations mentioned above.

Having given this brief overview of the excerpts in this section, we now review them in somewhat greater detail.

Intervening opportunities (Lathrop Hamburg)

The Lathrop Hamburg model may be considered as an alternative construct to the Lowry model which has not met with the same degree of acceptance. Developed at the Upstate New York Transportation Studies group, the central concept is that of intervening opportunities. Simply stated, this concept first asserts that a tripmaker will encounter alternative opportunities for satisfying his trip purpose as he travels. Second, it is asserted that there is a finite probability of the tripmaker's stopping at any one of these possible alternatives. Further, this probability increases, for each successive alternative, with each prior alternative not taken.

The implementation of this concept requires that a measure of opportunities be constructed for each zone in the region being modelled. In addition, some measure of zone-to-zone travel time or access must be constructed and, based on this, each zone must be rank-ordered, according to this measure, from each other zone. It then becomes a rather straightforward matter to calculate the probabilities of trips terminating at any other zone from each given origin.

The opportunities measure used in the model was the product of the available land and the obtaining density of activity, both of which were exogenous inputs, though there is a provision for calculating an endogenous density estimate. The allocation function used was:

$$A_j = A\left[e^{-lO} - e^{-l(O + O_j)}\right]$$

where

A_j = activities allocated to area j
A = total regional activity level
l = probability of a unity of activity siting at a given opportunity.
O = opportunities, rank ordered, and preceding zone j
O_j = opportunities in zone j.

The values of l were developed from analyses of base year data. It should be noted that the effect of l is to concentrate or disperse the regional pattern of activities. It can be seen from the allocation function that as l increases, each locating unity of activity will have a higher probability of locating at the first available opportunity. This behavior will lead to a centralization of location. Clearly then, as l decreases, one would expect to observe a decentralization of the region's activities.

The opportunities (i.e. zones containing them) are, as mentioned above, rank ordered from each origin. The ranking is based on some measure of the 'cost' of travelling from the given origin to each zone. The precise nature of the measure is not critical to the model construct and can be anything from airline distance to rather complex accessibility constructs. The general notion is that all the activities to be located from a given origin begin searching for opportunities to locate. The opportunities are encountered in the same sequence as their rankings, and at each opportunity (i.e. zone containing them) some portion of the locating activities from the given region will be located.

The model may be used for a complete allocation of activities over a previously 'empty' area as in the Lowry model. It can also be used as an incremental allocation procedure, allocating increments of activity to a base distribution. Like the Lowry model, this model is macro-descriptive and seems to be a reasonable construct for this sort of estimation. It has never, however, received the further testing, examination, and modifications which followed upon the Lowry work. Wilson, however, has shown how it too may be derived from entropy maximizing principles.[1] The intervening-opportunities construct should not, however, be disregarded as an alternative or supplementary description of the development of urban location patterns.

Component models of residential development

To this point, all the models discussed (with the exception of BASS) have taken a macro or aggregated view of urban spatial phenomena and accomplished their spatial allocations with a single allocation procedure which, in some sense, summarized the effects of several phenomena generally held to be the underlying causes of household location. These phenomena include the action of landowners, developers, and potential residents, along with industry, public policy and the like. The UNC work, after considerable analyses of these residential location phenomena, first tested a series of macro-descriptive models (Chapin and Weiss). Based on these results and the initial 'micro' analyses a second set of descriptive models was proposed. These models attempted to explain residential development in terms of a linked landowner-developer-resident set of models. Yet the internal structure of each of these submodels does not resemble the sort of structure customarily associated with either urban economics or the macro-descriptive models discussed above.

Each of the intended models in the UNC package was to calculate, by

1. Wilson, A. G., *Entropy in Urban and Regional Planning*, Pion, London, 1970.

means of what they call discriminant functions, the probability that a given unit of land would undergo some transition, e.g. from unsubdivided to subdivided. The discriminant functions involve first calculating an index from a linear multiple regression equation and then using the indices in a logic function. The model for estimating the probability of subdivision as described in the second excerpt of this group (Kaiser).

Further efforts made attempts to link three models of this type, with a model each for landowner, land developer, and land consuming resident. In each of these submodels, a probability was calculated for each possible action. The landowner model predicted the probabilities of the land being subdivided or unsubdivided into various housing types. The consumer model predicted the probabilities that the site, given its development, would be consumed (occupied) by a member of a particular population group. The making of a forecast involved selecting the highest probability outcome for each unit of land. While the final results obtained from these models were not overwhelmingly accurate, they were good enough to recommend that this approach not be overlooked. The notion of modelling separate components of the residential development phenomenon continues to occupy the attention of researchers in the field.

Linear programming and land use

Another model construct which gives separate consideration to different components of the residential location phenomenon, though from quite a different point of view, is the Herbert-Stevens model. The original conception of the model derives from the Alonso economic theory of residential land use.[2] It differs from the Alonso work in allowing for a polycentric urban form, in contradistinction to the monocentric hypothesis which underlies most economic models of urban areas. Another way of stating this is that any operational model of residential location must be capable of dealing with a spatial distribution of employment opportunities while many theoretical economic models of urban areas assume all employment opportunities to be concentrated at the center of the area.

In general, the structure of the model involves the allocation of a set of land users (residents) to land in the region. This allocation is accomplished by a linear programming algorithm. The objective function in this allocation is the consumer surplus (the difference between the household's residential budget and their cost for a particular type of residence) of all

2. Alonso, W., *Location and Land Use*, Harvard University Press, Cambridge, Mass., 1964.

households in the system. The constraints in the system provide that the consumption of land does not exceed the available land, and that all households get located.

From the general form of the model, it is possible, by substituting various objective functions and/or constraint functions, and by investigating both the primal and dual solutions to the problem, to gain many insights into the possible functioning of the urban land market. For example, the original version of the model (Herbert and Stevens) assigns households to parcels of land and, simultaneously, determines the type of housing to be constructed on the parcels. An alternative form of the model might accept an exogenous description of the housing stock and then make an optimal assignment of households to the existing housing stock. The excerpt from the Harris article discusses these and other possibilities and some of their outcomes.

The Herbert-Stevens model has never had a successful full scale implementation. Much work has been done, however, which provides useful insight into the functioning of the urban residential land market.[3] Since the more recent development of the relationships between this work and the new entropy-maximizing formulations, the results of the work with the Herbert-Stevens model have assumed greater significance for future work on the urban residential location problem.[4]

Other models not excerpted

Despite the already overlong list of models and excerpts included in this book, many others were omitted. Some of these omissions are due to the simple fact of the work not adding appreciably to what has been already presented. Some others may be due to the work simply never having been described in a public document or even a semi-public document and thus being unknown to this author. Other work had been presented in a form which simply seemed intractable insofar as presenting a lucid description of the work in excerpt form. Nonetheless, these exceptions were minor in comparison to the overall importance and quantity of the work which is included. The reader who takes the time to become familiar with the work presented here will have a very comprehensive overview of the development of urban residential simulation models leading up to the new work of the early 1970's.

3. Harris, B., J. Nathanson, and L. Rosenberg, 'Research on an Equilibrium Model of Metropolitan Housing,' University of Pennsylvania, Phila., Pa., 1966.
4. Wilson, A. G., and M. L. Senior, 'Some Relationships Between Entropy Maximizing Models, and their Duals', *Journal of Regional Science*, Vol. 14, no. 2, (1972) pp. 207–215.

4.2. OPPORTUNITY ACCESSIBILITY MODEL FOR ALLOCATING REGIONAL GROWTH

George T. Lathrop, J. R. Hamburg,
and G. F. Young

Highway Research Record No. 102 (1965) pp. 54–66

Concept of the model

The model is an opportunity model. In essence, the spatial distribution of an activity is viewed as the successive evaluation of alternative opportunities for sites which are rank ordered in time from an urban center. Opportunities are defined as the product of available land and density of activity (units of activity per unit area of land):

$$A_j = A\left[e^{-lO} - e^{-l(O + O_j)}\right]$$

where

$A_j =$ amount of activity to be allocated to zone j,
$A =$ aggregate amount of activity to be allocated,
$l =$ probability of a unit of activity being sited at a given opportunity,
$O =$ opportunities for siting a unit of activity rank ordered by access value and preceding zone j, and
$O_j =$ opportunities in zone j.

Clearly, the use of the negative exponential formulation following an access search across an opportunity surface presumes that the settlement rate per unit of opportunity is highest at the point of maximum access or, most usually, the center of a region. This presumption is elementary and agrees well with both empirical observations and the bulk of the theory dealing with the economics of land use.

An example of the empirical relationship was observed in the Niagara Frontier illustrating the regularity of the relationship between activity and opportunities for siting that activity when arranged in access (minimum time path value) order. These curves translated to the probability statement form the basis for the model.

Notion of opportunities

The concept of an opportunity for siting a unit of activity involves both land and a measure of the intensity of use of that land. Land-use intensity or density has been treated as an equilibrium of the price of land and transport costs.

An historical analysis of density must consider changing transportation costs, changing building costs with particular emphasis on the costs of first floor area vs. multistoried floor area, and changing requirements or preferences for location among competing activities. In addition to the difficulties that these considerations impose, there is the problem of structural rigidity of the physical region in terms of buildings and transportation facilities. These represent substantial investments which change only slowly.

Largely because of the difficulties involved in simulating the intensity of land use, we have chosen to utilize the present density as an appropriate measure which is independently introduced into the model. This independence allows the use of alternative densities whether analytically derived, guessed, or planned. We would naturally prefer to have these values generated with the model utilizing an algorithm which would simulate the competitive processes that establish land-use intensity. This remains as an area to be resolved in future work on the model.

Notion of probability of siting

The parameter *l* is the probability that a unit of activity will settle or be sited at a unit opportunity. For a given surface of opportunities, the larger this value, the more tightly packed the region will be. The smaller the value of *l*, the more scattered or sprawling the settlement pattern will be. Thus, it is a measure which describes, within the constraint of the density-land opportunity surface, the relative importance of central positioning within the region.

The model distributes growth increments across an opportunity surface which has been rank ordered by time path value to the center. After each increment of growth is allocated, the available land is reduced by the land required to site the increment of activity, the opportunity surface is decreased, and the activity inventory by zone is updated. Ignoring for the moment competing activities, the use of an *l* with large values would tend to settle each unit of activity at the first opportunity encountered. Thus, growth would simply be a process of completely using land in ever-increasing bands of access from the center. Very small values of l, on the other hand, would tend to scatter activity across the region. Although the center would still dominate and act as a center, the pattern of settlement would be very sparse. As l approaches zero, the notion of a region simply disappears.

There appears to be some general historical correspondence to a decreasing l, presumably as a result of changes in the transportation technology (especially the widespread use of the automobile). Thus, the transition from rural to urban was more abrupt in earlier cities. Land in a given time ring tended to be substantially used up before successive time rings would be settled. Currently, the demarcation is typically in a broad band which may be several miles in width.

An analysis of the Chicago population settlement pattern reveals a lessening of the slope of land saturation at increasing distances from the Loop through time.

Notion of access

The obvious impact of transport costs on the development of a region has long been recognized. The inclusion of some measure of accessibility into any model proposed to simulate present growth or estimate future growth is imperative. However, the form and weight that access should have in the model are not so obvious; in fact, this is the major area which requires clarification.

We have started from a simplified notion that growth begins at a center and proceeds outward. The supply or surface of opportunities for growth will be examined in order of the travel time required to reach any location on that surface. This concept is neither new nor especially unique.

In experimenting with our model prototype, we found that the settlement pattern was very sensitive to the transportation facilities. For example, a simple grid of facilities with equal speeds gives a square settlement pattern rotated 45° with respect to the grid. If the central X and Y dimension facilities have a speed advantage over the other facilities, the sides of the square are pulled in, and the settlement pattern approaches the shape of a four-pronged starfish. Some of our midwestern plains cities do, in fact, correspond to just this pattern or are first cousins thereof.

If only a single facility has the high-speed characteristic, the linear form of the city emerges. This is common to cities which fall in a valley with the main street running parallel to the ridges. Here, of course, the topography itself (in the form of the opportunity surface) tends to re-inforce the linear form of this settlement pattern.

The notion of access, developed here, should not be confused with the accessibility notion wherein a given location is related to all other locations by the sum of the quotients formed by each location's activity divided by its time or distance to the given zone raised to some power. This gravity or pro-pensity for interaction notion of access is a distinctly different measure. We have included an option for calculating this measure within our model. To date, we have not compared the results of using this alternative measure of access.

The major point we wish to make here is that by borrowing the minimum path capabilities of the existing assignment packages, we can order the opportunity surface by a much more refined measure than air line distance to the CBD. Thus, within the limitations of our allocation algorithm, we can incorporate the effects which specific transportation improvements would have on the settlement pattern. We are then in a much better position to handle the knotty question of feedback between land use and the transportation system.

4.3. SOME INPUT REFINEMENTS FOR A RESIDENTIAL MODEL

F. S. Chapin Jr. and
Shirley F. Weiss

Center for Urban and Regional Studies,
University of North Carolina.
July 1965

This provides a summary report on a sequence of investigations con-cerned with the design and calibration of a synthetic model for simulating residential growth. These investigations have had a strong methodological emphasis. A requirement of the work throughout has been to develop an operational approach to simulating the conversion of open land into resi-dential development in a form which could become a part of a larger system of land use models in transportation planning studies. The approach chosen makes use of a Monte Carlo type of probabilistic model and is designed to simulate residential development on an aggregate basis.

The first report, issued in August 1962 and entitled *Factors Influencing Land Development*, identified components for such a model and set forth the initial design. The second, issued in May 1964 and entitled *A Probabilistic Model for Residential Growth*, in effect was a mock-up of the model. In that study we carried the design to a test stage, putting to use analyses of variables made in the first study and reporting on the initial tests. The present monograph reports on a 'cleaned-up' version of the model.

As in the earlier tests, Greensboro, North Carolina, with a metropolitan area 1965 population of about 150,000 is the test city.[1] The data inputs are recorded in terms of a system of 1,000 by 1,000-foot grid squares and coded to subunit ninths (or subgrid squares $333\frac{1}{3}$ feet on a side). They are recorded for three-year growth periods during the time span 1948 to 1960.

The conceptual framework for this model focuses on the flow of actions which generate land development in an urban setting. It draws on an elemental behavior construct in which land development can be conceived as a kind of third-order outcome of a line of human action set in motion by man's effort to accommodate to his environment. In the most elemental form of this framework, the first-order concern is with *value systems* formed from man's experience with his environment – here, an urban one. The second-order area of analysis focuses on *behavior patterns* – the various kinds of human activities involved in city life which have become sufficiently routinized to take the form of definite patterns. There are many ways of studying urban activities, but one approach which has significance for this research is particularly concerned with patterns in spatial distribution and patterns of time allocated to activities. But to investigate these patterns is also to investigate antecedent values of at least two kinds – values with respect to environmental qualities and values placed on accessibility as it inhibits or facilitates the capability of an individual to engage in activities. These value considerations and activity patterns are seen to generate *location decisions*, the third-order area of concern in this framework. Here, the market mechanism, operating within constraints set by public policy, is seen to be the medium by which location behaviors respond to value systems and behavior patterns. It is this third-order or location aspect of the framework which is of direct concern in the model discussed below. In a highly simplified form the model

---

1. For detailed statement, see F. Stuart Chapin, Jr., and Shirley F. Weiss, *Factors Influencing Land Development*, An Urban Studies Research Monograph, Institute for Research in Social Science, University of North Carolina, Chapel Hill, in cooperation with the Bureau of Public Roads, U.S. Department of Commerce, August 1962.

simulates transactions in the market place within constraints set by city hall to effect a distribution of residential development.

Accordingly, within this broad framework, the first and second areas of analysis are held constant, and the model developed in this series of investigations simulates the end result of location decisions which occur in the third area of analysis. This aggregative approach to the residential growth process is seen to involve two sets of actions. One set, called 'priming actions', is made up of decisions affecting the location of a major new employment center, an expressway, a system of elementary schools, or an important sewer outfall or pumping station. Priming actions are seen to trigger the other set of actions, 'secondary actions' – in this case, a combination of housing decisions producing residential development.

The present model does not generate priming actions but rather simulates the final outcome of the primary-secondary action sequence. The priming actions are 'givens', and the question is asked: Given these priming actions, what secondary actions, that is, what residential development will occur? The given priming actions may be supplied as prescriptive inputs consisting of structuring elements taken directly from one or more alternative proposed general development schemes for the metropolitan area, or they may be outputs from a set of recursive growth models operating in tandem with this residential model. In either case, the output is the pattern of residential growth resulting from the composite of all housing location decisions taking into account the aggregate effect of priming actions. Under this simplified version of location behavior, the task of the model is to simulate the residential development pattern considering the attractiveness for development of all the various available sites and the changes in this attractiveness occasioned by certain scheduled priming actions.

Pursuant to this view of the household location process, the refined version of the model consists of the following steps:

1. The computer inputs the inventory of undeveloped land previously analyzed and coded for use capability. This inventory consists of two kinds; vacant subdivided land and open tracts. This step consists essentially of introducing a baseline description of land available and usable for residential development in the city as it exists at the beginning of a growth cycle.
2. For each unit suitable for residential use, a measure of relative value is assigned to it. For these purposes, assessed land values are used to establish a measure of attractiveness for residential development that

each grid unit possesses relative to all others before the growth process begins.
3. The effect that priming actions (selected programed public improvements and anticipated changes in employment concentrations) will have in modifying the relative value of land for residential use is then estimated.
4. Density and housing-value constraints imposed by the zoning ordinance and the operations of the land market are introduced, and land is 'reassessed' to obtain the total attractiveness of undeveloped areas for residential use, considering their initial value and the estimated adjustments in these values brought about by priming actions. The inventory of available land consists of ten density-value classes for each of the subdivided and the open land categories.
5. Finally, households in the market for each class of housing during the growth period (expressed in units of land to be pre-empted by new development) are allocated on a probabilistic basis.

This is the basic sequence in each of the four growth periods used in calibrating the model. The same sequence would be followed in projections into the future from the threshold date (in this model, 1960). Besides a number of simplifying steps in data preparation, the present refined model has been designed to simulate more closely the conditions encountered in the urban land market. In contrast to the initial version of the model which dealt with land only by density classes (four in all), it now differentiates between subdivided and raw land, and it operates on an inventory of ten density-value classes within each of these two categories, differing economic circumstances and varying density preferences.

The introduction of these changes points the way to an upcoming second generation system of location models. In breaking out the land inventory into subdivided and unsubdivided land, the first step has already been made in disaggregating the residential development process into two basic kinds of component processes: (1) subdivision developer actions (a producer model), and (2) household actions (a consumer model). Eventually, then, we foresee two linked models superseding the present aggregative model. The producer model would take account of the priming factors of the kind involved in the present model, evaluate the attractiveness of raw land for development, and then simulate developer behavior in the acquisition of parcels, the subdivision of land, and the construction of housing for selected consumer markets. The consumer model would operate on the inventory of housing created by the producer model and simulate the behavior of households in these selected consumer markets, with their selection of homesites being regulated by at least three kinds of factors: (1) the cost of the shelter package, (2) the accessibilities the site offers with respect to activity opportunities important to households in this market, and (3) the living qualities the shelter package and its location offer relative to household preference patterns in this market. Clearly the upcoming changes cut across all three levels of the conceptual framework outlined above, with the first and second level areas of investigation supplying inputs for models in the third level or location aspect of the conceptual framework.

Deviations from actual growth

Taking the median run, the distribution of deviations was examined for all residential cells. Over four-fifths of the deviations occurred in cells receiving one- or two-ninths of development below or above the absolute growth observed between 1948 and 1960. [See table 1.]

TABLE 4.3.1   Deviations between assigned growth and actual growth, by cell, median run 42, test series 2.

	Underallocation			Overallocation	
Deviation	Number of cells	Percent	Deviation	Number of cells	Percent
−9	1	0.1	+9	1	0.1
−8	4	0.5	+8	0	0.0
−7	5	0.6	+7	10	1.2
−6	7	0.8	+6	8	1.0
−5	19	2.2	+5	32	3.9
−4	31	3.6	+4	32	3.9
−3	79	9.2	+3	71	8.7
−2	174	20.2	+2	206	25.2
−1	540	62.8	+1	457	55.9

The cells having high deviations, that is, under- or overallocation of six ninths or more per cell, were selected for further examination. In this group of deviant cells, there were 17 cells with underallocation and 19 cells with overallocation. An initial check was made on the consistency of high deviation per cell in the first 10 consecutive runs. By process of elimination, the number of high underallocation cells was reduced to 12 and high overallocation cells to six. These 'hard-core' deviant cells were rechecked for consistency in the last 10 consecutive runs and none was eliminated this time.

Re-examination of all the variables included in the model for possible explanation of the overall pattern of deviation resulted in the following possibilities:

Possible explanations for underallocation
1. Assessed value for base year may not be representative of full 12-year test period. If there were no change in priming factors, the possibility of reassessment would be eliminated in Test Series 2.
2. Change in land value during the test period might occur in variables not covered by the priming factors, such as upgrading of neighborhoods by private or public renewal, or by changes in the character of contiguous development.
3. Developer 'know how' and scale of operation might generate development in clusters beyond that 'normally' indicated by the prevailing growth rate.
4. Land could be forced on the market beyond the normal expectation of the amount of vacant land going into the subdivision inventory.
   a. by managerial decision of company holding extensive inventory, to dispose of land or to develop sections in keeping with corporate fiscal policy;
   b. by estate sale, at negotiated price;
   c. by forced decision of overcommitted owner, at sacrifice price;
   d. by tax considerations, such as periodic reassessment practice, at low competitive price; or
   e. by buyer's determination to obtain specific holding for reasons not entirely related to market considerations, at high bid price.

Possible explanations for overallocation
1. Some subdivided land may not be appealing and should be downgraded to an intermediate inventory class. This might include:
   a. rural subdivisions without improvements
   b. 25-foot-lot subdivisions sparsely developed
   c. 'loser' subdivisions, i.e. wrong location for nuisance reasons, aesthetic considerations, downgrading of contiguous neighborhoods, or lack of 'know how' of the developer
2. Suitable vacant land withheld from residential development because of ownership pattern, designation for future nonresidential use, speculative considerations, or ethnic practices.

While the foregoing list was screened for the plausibility of these explanations, additional research and study would be required before acceptance
or rejection of any one of the explanations would be warranted.

4.4. A PRODUCER MODEL FOR RESIDENTIAL GROWTH

Edward J. Kaiser

Center for Urban and Regional Studies,
University of North Carolina Chapel Hill.
November 1968

A planning approach to the model

The Model is intended for use in the field by planners interested in anti-
cipating the location of residential growth on the urban fringe and in
influencing its spatial pattern. Hence, we have taken a planning-oriented
approach by suggesting an operational (i.e. workable) model that is 'future
predictive' and 'conditionally predictive'.

By an operational 'future predictive' model we mean to distinguish it
from one that might be called a conceptual model or theoretical model.
In a workable 'future predictive' model, the reliability of prediction of
future conditions in a relevant real world context is more important than a
conceptualized explanation of past or present conditions. Thus, while
our model might deemphasize explanation, it must detail the relationships
and it must fit parameters and empirical variables to the actual situations
relevant to planning. In other words, the predictive model with which we
are concerned must be empirically explicit but can be conceptually vague,
while the theoretical model must be conceptually explicit but can be
empirically vague. While we have tried to base our model on an explicit
and sound conceptual basis in order to make it more reliable and more
fruitful in its suggestiveness, we are in this chapter primarily concerned
with converting the research into a model of use in an empirical planning
situation.

By calling for a 'conditionally predictive' model we mean to distinguish
it from a forecast model.[1] The emphasis in the forecast model is on

1. For a fuller discussion of 'conditional prediction' see Ira S. Lowry, 'A Short Course in
Model Design,' a review article, *Journal of the American Institute of Planners*, vol. 31, no. 2,
May 1965, p. 159 and Britton Harris, 'New Tools for Planning', *Journal of the American
Institute of Planners*, vol. 31, no. 2, p. 91, May 1967.

simplicity of structure, feasibility of input, and sharpness of prediction based on predetermined input. It is satisfactory for a prediction which the planner does not seek to control but merely requires as an item of information for planning. An example might be a population projection for land use planning where the planner is not using the projections to influence or control the population growth but rather as input information for land use planning decisions. On the other hand, the spatial distribution of residential subdivisions is a model output which the planner does wish to influence, if not control. When dealing with the spatial distribution of residential growth therefore the planner requires models which aid in tracing the effects of contemplated planning courses of action posed as conditions – hence the term, conditional. The emphasis is on the model's 'if ... then' prediction capabilities where planning implementation instruments play the role of at least some of the 'if's'. Thus we desire variables on the predictor side of the model's equations that are able to reflect implementation instruments.

The more specifically stated purpose of the workable, future and conditionally predictive model is limited to the prediction of the spatial variation in likelihood of single family residential subdivisions in an urban study area for some future finite period of time, say 3–10 years. It is not an allocation model at this point, i.e. it does not actually spatially distribute an exogeneously determined amount of subdivision growth. Its main purpose is to identify areas most likely to receive subdivision. It does this on the basis of the spatial distribution of site characteristics in the urban area at the beginning of the period. The site characteristics used in this pilot version are the same as those introduced earlier:

Physical characteristics
    Proportion of marginal land
    Proportion of poor soil
Local characteristics
    Socio-economic rank
    Distance to central business district
    Distance to nearest major street
    Distance to nearest elementary school
    Accessibility to employment areas
    Amount of contiguous residential development
Institutional characteristics
    Availability of public utilities
    Zoning protection

Other characteristics may be more useful in other study areas, these may be measured differently, or they may refer to differently defined zones. The site characteristics may represent an actual situation or they may represent a planning hypothesis – a sort of 'suppose the site characteristics were .... ' hypothesis. At least some of the site characteristics must be capable of reflecting governmental actions such as zoning, service districts, and capital improvements to provide for conditional prediction. The future impact of either an existing situation, a forecasted situation, or a planning supposition may be tested by channeling its impact first through the spatial distribution of site characteristics and then through the empirically calibrated relationships to influence the spatial pattern of subdivisions.

Description of the model

The model requires certain prerequisites. Required at the outset (as an input) is a description of the metropolitan area as it exists or is hypothesized at the start of the growth period. This includes a description of the availability of land for development and the physical, locational, and institutional characteristics of the land.[2] Secondly, if the model is to be used over a succession of time periods or to test alternative land development policies, an exogenous modification of the site characteristics to reflect their change over time or to reflect the impact of hypothesized policies would be required. Thirdly, the model requires that the appropriate variables be measured and coded for some system of zones in the urban area (that is, the value of each property characteristic be recorded for each zone) and that the information be recorded on punched cards or magnetic tape.

For each zone (unit of area) in the input data set, the model calculates a probability for each of the set of mutually exclusive outcomes (categories) possible for the zone. For example, if the model was being applied to determine 'subdivided vs. unsubdivided' it would determine the probability

---

2. An option exists also for the input of the propensity of predevelopment landowner to sell taken from the output of the predevelopment landowner sub-model preceding the land developer model in the system of models. The use of this option would necessarily accompany the use of the developer model as one link in the chain-like system of linked models but is optional when the developer model is used by itself. As an example of a predevelopment landowner model link which generates relative propensity to sell see Edward J. Kaiser, *et al.* 'Predicting the Behavior of Predevelopment Landowners on the Urban Fringe', *Journal of the American Institute of Planners*, vol. 34, no. 5, September 1968.

of subdivision occurring in the zone and the probability of the zone not receiving subdivision. These probabilities are determined by the discriminant model as a function of the vector of predictor property characteristics for that zone.

The coefficients for the discriminant functions used in the model must be supplied by the planner-modeler. Ordinarily these coefficients will have been determined through a discriminant analysis performed on a data set the planner believes to be relatively similar to the one to which the model will be applied. Most often this so-called calibration of the model should probably de done on a relatively recent sample from the same urban area.

After the probabilities are determined for all zones there are several possible options: (a) the list of probabilities can be considered to be the output of the model and can be produced on a printout and/or (b) these probabilities together with corresponding locations of zones can provide the input for a computer mapping program which in turn can organize the output into a map showing the spatial distribution of the probabilities for some selected category of outcome.

Operation of the model

The operation of the model will be described as it is applied to a set of test data in Greensboro. The description will show how the model takes in data representing Greensboro in 1960 and using this data produces a forecast of the spatial distribution tendencies of subdivision in the period 1961 through 1963.

The program draws in one record of data at a time representing all relevant data for one zone. Thus we can begin by drawing in the first record (zone) of the Greensboro data set. The variables in the record describe its location and the pertinent site characteristics of the zone as of 31 December, 1960. More specifically, in attempting to forecast subdivisions without regard to developer type of price range, each record would contain at least the following data:

1. The x and y coordinates of the location of the zone in the metropolitan area. These data can be used later to map the outcomes, but they play no role in calculating the outcome.
2. The values of the predictor variables determined from earlier analysis to influence the location of subdivision. In our example we read in:
   a. $x_3 = $ the socio-economic rank of the location

b. x_5 = distance to the nearest elementary school
c. x_6 = an index of accessibility to employment areas
d. x_9 = availability of public utilities and services (water, and sanitary sewer facilities, police and fire protection).

These were the variables which were indicated to be important for our purposes by an analysis of data for an earlier (1958–1960) period. If we were interested in forecasting only large developer subdivisions or some other category of subdivision, the list might be different.

Using the data from the record (zone) just read in, the program assigns a probability to each possible outcome category using discriminant functions calibrated on test data of an earlier period. These are, of course, the same test data that determined which site characteristics we read in as predictors. The general form of the discriminant functions in the model (one function for each dependent category) is given by:

$$F_i(x_1, x_2, \ldots, x_m) = c_{0,i} + \sum_{j=1}^{m} c_{i,j} x_j$$

for $i = 1, 2, \ldots, g$ and $j = 1, 2, \ldots, m$

where

g = number of dependent outcome categories (groups)
m = number of independent predictor variables.
The coefficients, $c_{0,i}$ and $c_{i,j}$ are supplied by the planner-modeler as parameters in the program and come from calibration of the function on test data. For each outcome category i (and for each observation) a probability is calculated as follows:

$$P_i = \frac{\exp(f_i - \max f_i)}{\sum_i \exp(f_i - \max f_i)}$$

In our example we would have two such probabilities calculated for each zone:

$$P_{\text{unsub}} = \frac{\exp(f_{\text{unsub}} - \max f_i)}{\exp(f_{\text{unsub}} - \max f_i) + \exp(f_{\text{subdiv}} - \max f_i)}$$

and

$$P_{\text{subdiv}} = \frac{\exp\left(f_{\text{subdiv}} - \max f_j\right)}{\text{(same denominator)}}$$

These probabilities as well as the name of the outcome category having the largest probability, P, is noted and stored. The next record is read in and the same calculations and classifications are made. This continues through the last zone. At this point the program allows the planner-modeler to select one or both of two options. The first option is to print out a list consisting of probabilities and the outcome having the largest probability for each zone for which input data was supplied to the program. Such a printout may be studied by the planner directly. Or the results could be mapped by a draftsman, by referring to the x-y coordinate location of the zone if that is given or some other identification such as census tract number.

4.5. A MODEL FOR THE DISTRIBUTION OF RESIDENTIAL ACTIVITY IN URBAN AREAS

**John D. Herbert and
Benjamin H. Stevens**

Journal of Regional Science, vol. 2, no. 2, 1960

Introduction

The model presented here is designed to distribute households to residential land in an optimal configuration. The model was constructed for the Penn-Jersey Transportation Study as part of a larger model designed to locate all types of land-using activity.

Since the model had to be suitable for practical application a certain amount of conceptual elegance has been sacrificed in favor of operational simplicity. The larger model operates in the following way: The total relevant time period is subdivided into a number of short iterative periods. For each iterative period different types of land-using activity are handled separately. A particular type of activity is distributed in a configuration that is optimal only with respect to all previously located activities.[1]

---

1. For a particular type of activity in a particular iterative period, previously located activities comprise all activities located in previous periods plus activities of other types previously located (by other elements in the larger model) in the same period.

Interactions that are expected to occur among simultaneously-locating activities are ignored.

We are assuming that they can be ignored if iterative periods are kept short enough to ensure that the number of users located in a single run of the model is small. Operating in this way we are able to achieve computational simplicity and, at the same time, recognize most of the basic interactions among land users.[2]

For the residential model, in a particular iterative period, the number of households to be located and the amount of land that is expected to be available for residential use is forecast exogenously.[3] A linear program is used to produce, for the end of that period, an optimal configuration of the new households on the available land. This configuration is optimal with respect to the configuration of all previously located activities, and constitutes a prediction of the way in which the forecast households will locate....[4]

Conceptual framework

We assume that the factors which a household considers in choosing an area in which to locate are its total budget, the items which constitute a market basket, and the costs of obtaining those items. For each household group we posit a set of market baskets among which each household in that group is 'indifferent'.[5] We posit the set which includes, but is not neces-

2. For example, if we take an extreme case with an iterative period of one week, the number of land users that will be located in that period is likely to be small; it seems reasonable, both conceptually and realistically, to assume that they will make their locational decisions largely independent of one another. However, interactions between users located in a particular week and those located in previous weeks will be recognized, with the result that a vast majority of the important interactions are taken into account. For Penn-Jersey we envisage an interative period of at least a year, which will certainly introduce inaccuracies; but we can achieve any level of accuracy that we desire, at the cost of increasing computational complexity, by decreasing the length of the periods.
3. The residential model can handle land that is vacant, partially improved, or completely built-up. For expositional simplicity, the discussion will be limited to vacant land unless otherwise noted. Forecasts are exogenous in the sense that they are made outside the overall model (by techniques that are beyond the scope of the present discussion) but can be modified for a particular iterative period to recognize the configurations produced by the model in previous periods.
4. Linear programming is not ordinarily regarded as a predictive tool. However, if we have a prediction of the number of households that is to be located and the model locates them in a realistic configuration then we can use the model to predict configurations. Since the configurations it produces are optimal in a specific economic sense the model may be both predictive and prescriptive.
5. The household is 'indifferent' among the baskets only in a limited sense which will be made clear in the subsequent discussion.

sarily limited, to the market baskets currently consumed by households of that type.[6] We permit the household to opetimize, not by selecting a market basket from *all* the conceivable sets from which it could obtain satisfaction, but by selecting from the posited set the market basket which maximizes that household's 'savings'.

These 'savings' arise in the following way. A household has a fixed total budget. For a particular market basket the prices of the items in the 'other commodities' bundle are given. The residential budget is therefore a residual determined by the size of the total budget and the cost of the 'other commodities' bundle. Clearly, it may vary from market basket to market basket. Notice that the character of each of the four items that constitute a residential bundle may vary from market basket to market basket also. Each market basket in the indifference set will have in it a unique residential bundle which has a unique residential budget associated with it. Disregarding site for a moment, the costs of each of the other three items in a residential bundle may vary from area to area. For a particular area, the difference between the residential budget assigned to a particular residential bundle and the cost of the bundle exclusive of the site in it is the maximum amount the household can pay in that area for that site. And it will be the maximum amount that the landowner could extract from the household as site rent. If land were free, it would be a measure of the savings enjoyed by the household because of the household's rent-paying ability for that site in that area.

Although we have said that a household is 'indifferent' among the market baskets in its indifference set, it seems reasonable to suppose that such savings would have a positive marginal utility for the household. Therefore, in the model, a rational household will attempt to obtain from its indifference set the market basket in which those 'savings' are a maximum. In reality, the functioning of land market may make it possible for the landowner to draw off the 'savings' as rent. Nevertheless, the attempt of each household to maximize its savings will result in house-

6. This is based on the assumption that households have, in the past, come close to achieving optimal levels of satisfaction. However, where empirical evidence suggests that market imperfections have precluded optimization we can add to the indifference set market baskets that could be chosen by the household in a market free of imperfections. Obviously there are conceptual weaknesses involved in the use of empirical evidence for the identification of indifference sets. We assume that it is possible to construct operationally acceptable sets that are based on such evidence without being tied rigidly to it. The model will not permit the indifference set that is relevant for a particular household to change during an iteration. But this does not preclude the possibility of allowing taste changes to occur from the iteration to another.

holds being allocated to land in configuration that is optimal from the point of view of all the households that are to be located. This allocation will be optimal in a Pareto sense: no household can move to increase its savings without reducing the savings of some other household and simultaneously reducing aggregate savings. Since we have made savings synonymous with rent-paying *ability*, an optimal allocation is achieved by the maximization of aggregate rent-paying ability.[7]

The primal problem

Notation:

U = areas which form an exhaustive subdivision of the region. Areas are indicated by the superscripts $K = 1, 2, \ldots, U$.

n = household groups indicated by subscripts $i = 1, 2, \ldots, n$.

m = residential bundles indicated by subscripts $h = 1, 2, \ldots, m$.

b_{ih} = is the residential budget allocated by a household of group i to the purchase of residential bundle h.

c_{ih}^K = is the annual cost to a household of group i of the residential bundle h in area K, exclusive of site cost.

s_{ih} = is the number of acres in the site used by a household of group i if it uses residential bundle h.

L^K = is the number of acres of land available for residential use in area K in a particular iteration of the model.

N_i = is the number of households of group i that are to be located in the region in a particular iteration.

X_{ih}^K = is the number of households of group i using residential bundle h located, by the model, in area K.

The allocation model

The primal linear programming model for allocating households to land

7. In a Henry Georgian single-tax economy, the maximization of aggregate rent-paying ability would provide a maximization of public revenue. In a socialist system, if land were free, maximization of aggregate rent-paying ability would provide a maximization of consumer's surplus.

has the rather simple form:[8]

$$\text{Maximize } Z = \sum_{K=1}^{U} \sum_{i=1}^{n} \sum_{h=1}^{m} X_{ih}^{K}(b_{ih}^{K} - C_{ih}^{K}) \qquad (1.0)$$

subject to:

$$\sum_{i=1}^{n} \sum_{h=1}^{m} s_{ih} X_{ih}^{K} \leqq L^{K} \qquad (K = 1, 2, \ldots, U) \qquad (1.1)$$

$$\sum_{K=1}^{U} \sum_{h=1}^{m} -X_{ih}^{K} = -N_{i} \quad (i = 1, 2, \ldots, n) \qquad (1.2)$$

and all $X_{ih}^{K} \geqq 0$
$$\qquad (K = 1, 2, \ldots, U)$$
$$\qquad (i = 1, 2, \ldots, n)$$
$$\qquad (h = 1, 2, \ldots, m)$$

Constraints (1.1) prevent the consumption of land in each area from exceeding the land available. Constraints (1.2) require the model to locate the projected numbers of households of each group. These constraints are equalities because inequalities (of either sense) would not fit the overall requirements of the model. Suppose these constraints were written in such a way that the model was prevented from locating more than the projected numbers of households. This would be logical since we are interested in the situation where a particular number of households are located, not where the model can continue locating households in unlimited numbers until all the available land is used up. However, it is just as logical to write the constraints in such a way that the model is required to locate at least the projected numbers of households. This is particularly important where there are household groups which have negative or zero rent-paying ability in all areas. Without constraint, the model would choose not to locate these households at all since at best they would not add to, and at worst they would subtract from, aggregate rent-paying ability. For these reasons it is difficult to establish a general rule for the sense of

8. Although there are Umn variables to be determined, it is possible to eliminate many of them in advance of the computation of the program. We can do this for each household in each area by disregarding all residential bundles that yield less than the maximum unit rent-paying ability for that household in that area. These would have to be eliminated in any case in the process of maximization; a prior removal of them can reduce computational time and effort considerably.

the inequalities. Therefore it is preferable, and perfectly reasonable to make the constraints equalities.[9] The objective function (1.0) to be maximized is, of course, aggregate rent-paying ability.

Households may be allocated to land in the following ways: (1) One type of household may use all the land available in an area. This will occur where that type of household can yield the highest unit rent for the land in the area and there is a sufficient number of such households to fill the area. (2) The land available in an area may not be used up entirely. Partial utilization will occur where the area has strong locational advantages for only one of the household groups and there are not enough households of this type to fill the area, or where the area has strong locational advantages for two or more household groups and these groups, in toto, cannot fill the area. (3) The available land in an area may be left vacant if all households have higher unit rent-paying abilities in other areas and can find sites in other area. (4) The land available in an area may be used by more than one type of household. This will occur where there are not enough households in the group with the highest unit rent-paying ability in the area to fill that area and they are joined by other households with unit rent-paying abilities the same as, or lower than, the highest group but higher in this area than in other areas. Joint utilization can occur also in the unusual circumstance where two or more household groups have identical unit rent-paying abilities in the area and in all other areas where they could outbid other groups for sites.[10]

The dual of the allocation model

The notation of the dual problem is identical to that of the primal except

9. Actually, it is more likely to be necessary to force the model to locate households with zero or negative rent-paying ability than to restrict the number of households which may be located. This is reflected in the minus signs which appear on both sides of constraints (1.2). If these constraints were written as inequalities they would read:

$$\sum_{h=1}^{m} \sum_{K=1}^{u} X_{ih}^{K} < N_i.$$

But without the minus signs the inequalities would be of the opposite sense. In a maximization problem the inequalities must be of the '<' form. Therefore the minus signs are necessary. They could be removed when constraints (1.2) are changed to equalities. But the interpretation of the dual variables is somewhat easier if the minus signs are left in the primal.

10. This is the degenerate case in which there is no unique optimal allocation of the households in the groups which fulfill this condition. A further degenerate case can occur where a particular household group has the same unit rent-paying ability in a number of areas, none of which it can fill completely.

that the solution variables, X_{ih}^K are replaced by:

r^K = the annual rent per unit of land area K. ($K = 1, 2, \ldots, U$)
v_i = the annual subsidy per household for all households of group i. ($u = 1, 2, \ldots, n$) The use and meaning of the subsidy variables will be made clear below.

The dual problem is to minimize:

$$Z' = \sum_{K=1}^{U} r^K L^K + \sum_{i=1}^{n} v_i(-N_i) \tag{2.0}$$

subject to:

$$s_{ih} r^K - v_i \geq b_{ih} - c_{ih}^K \quad (K = 1, 2, \ldots, U), (i - 1, 2, \ldots, n) \tag{2.1}$$
$$(h = 1, 2, \ldots, m)$$

$$\text{all } r^K \geq 0 \quad (K = 1, 2, \ldots, U)$$

$$v_i \geq 0 \quad (j = 1, 2, \ldots, n).^{11}$$

In most linear programming models, the dual presents a problem in interpretation. The existence of the dual is a mathematical fact. But often it also contains information and provides insights which are as important as those provided by the primal itself. This is particularly true in the case of the present model. If we look at the objective function (2.0) and neglect for a moment the second summation, we can interpret the first summation as the total land rent.[12]

It may seem peculiar to minimize total land rent in the dual when we are maximizing aggregate rent-paying ability in the primal problem. It can be shown that the optimal solution of the primal problem must be exactly equal to the optimal solution of the dual. But there is also an important

---

11. An inequality (1.1) in the primal corresponds to a nonnegative variable r^K in the dual. But an equation (1.2) in the primal corresponds to a variable, v_i, whose sign is unrestricted in the dual. Thus the v_i, can be positive or negative.
12. The second summation is the total of 'subsidies' paid to households. We will see later how these subsidies add to the rent-paying ability of households and thereby in the rental income of landowners. But notice that the total value of the subsidies is subtracted from the total land rent (and could, in fact, be taxed away from landowners without altering the optimal configuration). Therefore, the value Z to be minimized is actually net land rent.

economic interpretation of the dual objective. Suppose that all land in all areas is owned by a monopolist. Then the minimization of site rent will minimize the returns to this monopolist. Alternatively, land could be widely held by individual holders. We could then be minimizing returns to the rentier class as a whole. To put it another way, we are obtaining sites for households as cheaply as possible within the constraints of the model.

This is not necessarily a desirable goal if it causes inequities to land owners. But notice that the constraints (2.1) prevent the unit rent on each site from falling below the unit rent-paying ability of any household that might locate on that site.[13] This means that the individual landowner can receive at least as much per unit as the highest bidder for his land is willing to pay. This will create certain problems when the household group which can bid highest does not actually purchase the land because it has an even higher unit rent-paying ability elsewhere. It is this latter case, and certain other cases, in which the 'subsidy' variables become important.

Bear in mind that a household which can bid the highest unit rent in a particular area is not necessarily of the 'wealthiest' household group. Unit rent-paying ability depends upon both total rent-paying ability and size of site purchased. 'Poorer' households using small sites may be the highest bidders, per unit land, in a particular area. Thus 'subsidies' in the model, may be assigned in some cases to 'wealthy' households.

4.6. LINEAR PROGRAMMING AND THE PROJECTION OF LAND USES

Britton Harris

Penn Jersey Transportation Study, Paper No. 20
November 9, 1962

The Herbert-Stevens model

Herbert and Stevens proposed to allocate an increment of population to locations in the metropolitan area according to a linear programming scheme. In this scheme, the main advantage which a household achieves by selecting a particular location is some relative saving in transportation

---

13. Neglecting the v_i, we could divide both sides of (2.1) by s_{ih}. Then unit rent (on the left) must be no less than unit rent-paying ability (on the right). Since this must hold for every household-bundle combination in an area, it then must hold for the combination which would yield the highest unit rent.

costs. Additionally, it may find available in this area a housing type which is more or less satisfactory to it. For location involving any particular housing type anywhere in the area, a household type is willing to allocate a specified budget depending on its means and its preferences. In the Herbert-Stevens model, this budget covers all costs of location, including the cost of housing, of land, and of interaction. This budget is then reduced by the actual outlays which would have to be made for transportation, for house cost, and for amenity in any particular location. The deduction for amenity costs assumes that the amenity of the most desired area can at some cost be reproduced in the less desired areas. The residual, after deducting these costs from the budget, represents what the authors call 'rent-paying ability'. A more useful and accurate term might be 'land-rent bid price', or simply 'bid-rent'. It should be clear that the land-rent bid of some household types in some areas might be very low or even negative if their budgets are limited, or if the area is of low amenity to them, or if their location in this area incurs high transportation costs.

The essential feature of the Herbert-Stevens model is, then that the allocation of population to areas is such as to maximize the total rent-paying ability which is engaged in location, or the total land-rent bid (and 'accepted'). It is important to note that this criterion does not maximize rents paid, but actually minimizes them, as we discuss below. It also does not necessarily have any implications about the minimization of individual consumer satisfaction, since the budgets and land-rent bids are defined so that at the bid prices, every consumer is indifferent between all locations in the metropolitan area.

The implications of this model remain to be more fully explored, but this exploration cannot be undertaken without a brief description of some of the more important changes in the model.

PJ's modifications of the model

There are a number of definitional changes which are not trivial. We have redefined the areas of the Herbert-Stevens model in an arbitrary way for computational purposes. There are two levels of areas. The first level is a normal *geographic area* such as a transportation zone or district, within which many transportation aspects of location may be considered homogeneous. Within such an area there are subareas of homogeneous housing types or homogeneous land. The totality of homogeneous parcels of a certain class within any one transportation district, while not necessarily contiguous, is defined to be an area in the sense of the model, or a *model area.* Model areas have uniform locational *and* land-use qualities. It should be apparent that the size and extent of these arbitrarily defined areas will change over time as building and conversion of structures takes place.

The housing type which thus defines areas and which enters into households' preference structures is in turn defined to include not only a house of a given type and condition, but also a given quantity of land. Thus, a seven-room single-family development house on a quarter-acre of land is not, in principle, the same housing type as the same house on one acre of land.

The rent-paying abilities and rents which will be inputs and outputs of the locational model have been redefined for built-up areas to include both land rent and structure rent. As a matter of economic investigation, it is very difficult to provide a reliable separation of these magnitudes, and the performance of the model is not necessarily affected by this change of concept. In vacant land areas, the rent-paying ability and rents to be considered will be net of the house cost. In both built-up and vacant areas, the performance of the model will depend on the management of alternative uses of the land or structure. If prices (rents) for alternative uses can be entered realistically into the model, the land or structures will be left 'vacant' only when the alternative use has a higher rent-paying ability (that is, yields a greater return) than any locators being considered. In the handling of private redevelopment through demolition, this treatment is advantageous since such a process of redevelopment can occur only if for some purpose the value of vacant land in a geographic area is equal to or greater than the value of land plus buildings in developed portions of the same area.

A basic change in the application of the model which is in part definitional deals with household budgets and with the treatment of amenity. Instead of regarding amenity as a reproducible good which can be supplied to a site and which represents a deduction against a fixed budget, we deduct the Herbert-Stevens amenity costs from both sides of the equation. We propose to estimate budgets which reflect the households' evaluation of the amenity and convenience of location, site, and housing type. Budgets would thus be specific to household types, housing types, *and* areas. Once again it is possible to study this question directly, since the data for location budgets by these categories are in general available, while the fixed budgets which do not take account of area characteristics are an artificial construct. Since the deduction for lack of amenity is applied against the budget before it is entered into the model, there is no effect on the operation of the model by comparison with what would occur under the original Herbert-Stevens plan.

. . .the authors discuss the method for choosing the best housing type for a household type competing with other households in a given area. Within any built-up model area, no choice of housing type exists, except in the rare case where conversion in use is permitted, since the model areas are by definition homogeneous as to housing type. A much wider range of choices exists in the case of vacant land. Wherever such choices exist, cases may arise where the highest rent-paying ability per acre is not the correct criterion for the choice of housing type for a particular household type. This situation arises when one household type has a higher rent-paying ability per acre than any other household type and than the alternative use. If such a household type also has another and more extensive preferred housing type which still preserves its net advantage in rent-paying ability per acre, then these two housing types must be compared. The one which yields the higher *total* rent-paying ability per household should be selected for entering into the model.

Various considerations, including those discussed above, suggest the desirability of creating a dummy population type which refers to locators with uses outside of the current particular application of the model. This group, in total, must have unlimited demand. Thus, when residential location is being considered, farm, woodland, and industrial uses are outside the model, but they all offer a certain price of rent per acre of land in various areas. The highest of these offers from the previous application of the overall model may determine the price of the alternative use. In the case of vacant land, it would appear from the behavior of the market that even in identical uses, institutional and other factors distort this price structure. Not all farm land is equally available for development in any particular area at a given time. This problem of land release is critical to the realism of the model, since releasing too much land in inlying areas could result in excessively compact development. Rather than attempt to estimate precisely the amounts of land to be released and taken up, since this will be determined by the model, we plan to simulate the supply-curve of land in each area by a step function. Areas of homogeneous land will be subdivided into blocks at increasing offering prices or rents so that only when the pressure for development on an area becomes very great will all land be taken up.

It seems probable that this type of land-supply function may be used to evade the accumulation problem discussed near the end of the Herbert-Stevens paper. We restate this problem briefly. The model estimates rent-paying ability by deducting house costs and average travel costs from a locational budget. Near large subcenters in the metropolitan region at existing levels of development, average travel costs may be quite low. This has, in fact, been observed by *PJ* in Trenton, in Norristown, and in Chester. This would make these areas more attractive for location for certain groups. If, however, an excessive number of families of such groups were to locate in these areas, they would not find nearby employment and their average transportation costs would rise, making the area less attractive to them. To take account of this phenomenon in estimating trip lengths is a difficult and expensive procedure. In such localities, it is possible to limit the locational attractiveness by steepening the land-supply function discussed in the preceding paragraph. When this is done, the land-supply function becomes, in part, an artificial construct designed to facilitate the operation of the model.

The calculations needed to solve the linear program method proposed by Herbert and Stevens tend to be somewhat long. By breaking up the problem into several stages, these calculations may be shortened. A partitioning indicated by considerations of realism as well as by computational costs will be to make a separation between owners and renters in the housing market. The computations themselves will be speeded up by a method due to Dr. Stevens wherein the problem as formulated is reduced to a number of iterations of a much simpler linear programming problem, generally called the transportation problem.

The model and the market

We have stated that the Herbert-Stevens model attempts to simulate the operation of the housing market in the large metropolitan area. Having in mind the basic structure of the model and the modifications which have been made to it for application at *PJ*, we are now in a position to examine this function in somewhat more detail.

In the metropolitan land market, we assume for purposes of the analysis that every family has more or less evaluated all of the types of housing available in all of the geographic subareas of the region. With this evaluation in mind, families have established budgets which they are willing to allocate for each of these 'locational bundles'. At these budgeted prices, it is a matter of complete indifference to any household where it may locate. Any very strong preferences are already reflected in much higher budgeted offers. On the other hand, land and housing units for rent or for sale are held by property owners who insist on securing the highest possible prices for their properties. Through constant transactions, going prices for a tremendous variety of facilities and locations are continually being established and modified, and these prices maintain a fairly constant structure over time. At any particular point in time, therefore, a structure of rents and prices has been determined. Would-be locators adjust their budgetary allocations so that they are able to secure accommodations at these going prices. Suppliers of housing services and of land on which housing can be constructed follow one of a number of courses. Owners of existing housing, in order to avoid vacancies or to achieve a reasonably quick sale, set prices which are in line with going market prices since they are in competition with other property owners. In certain instances they alter or convert their properties so as to provide a different housing type which is known to command a higher total net rent. Holders of vacant land may, if zoning permits, develop it or allow it to be developed in the housing type which will provide the highest profit on the land, that is, the housing type which maximizes total ground rent. In a number of cases, however, a land owner who observes that prices are rising because of changes which are taking place in the market may elect to hold his property for speculative gains.

It is thus apparent that in the land market in general both landlords and consumers of housing are faced by an existing structure of prices to which they adjust their actions. In modeling the growth of a metropolitan area, however, the problem is to determine *de novo* the structure or changes of this price system, on the basis of the known budgets and preferences of locators and the known behavior of property owners, but without correct advance knowledge of the price structure. In this case, the behavior of locators and owners must be restated. Owners attempt to secure the highest possible price or rent. Locators attempt to secure a location at which their rent involves the highest negative or lowest positive displacement from their offering prices specified by their indifference surface. In general, property owners will attempt to avoid vacancies or a failure to dispose of their properties, while locators will generally insist on securing accommodations even if they must increase their expenditures to do so.

The linear programming formulation of the Herbert-Stevens model simulates precisely this type of competition. The solution is similar to or identical with the solution which would be arrived at by competition, and in general no one's situation can be improved without making someone else worse off. This type of solution is called a Pareto optimum. The solution has two further properties of interest for our purposes. As a result of the competition between landlords, the total of rents and prices paid is minimized. At the same time, the total transportation costs of locators are minimized, subject, however, to the condition that if a household prefers a location with higher transportation cost so much that it is willing to allocate those transportation costs in a higher budget, then it will secure the new location. The model would minimize transportation cost if households were indifferent between locations on grounds of amenity and housing type. As it is, therefore, it minimizes transportation costs subject to a pattern of preferences.

It must be emphasized in this description that the behavior of the model is not the same as the behavior of the consumer or of the market as a whole. The model merely produces the same final result as a certain type of market. While the model maximizes total rent-paying ability, the consumer does not ordinarily attain a maximum. He is simply located to his satisfaction. It seems that in very general terms this is a perfectly reasonable description of the land market. It is true that many people accept somewhat less than satisfactory arrangements in order to avoid the costs of moving. This contingency is taken care of by relocating only a portion of the population at each iteration. It is also true, however, that population groups may have an imperfect perception of the housing market, and this fact is not fully taken into account in the model. Also, in one iteration, it seems likely that the location of the population may be slightly more 'lumpy' and less mixed than what occurs in real life, owing to the fact that in general only one population group is assigned to one area.

5. Summary and prospects

5.1. INTRODUCTION

The evolution of these urban simulation models and their various successes and failures may be viewed from different perspectives. For the planner in an agency where one of the many unsuccessful attempts was made, such models may well be held in rather low esteem. In fairness, this is not an unreasonable position for such a person to take. Some economists have claimed that there was never any reason to expect that such models should work, as they (the models) were lacking a proper economic foundation. Although somewhat gratuitous, neither is this assertion wholly false. Other professionals, both planners and model builders, will claim many virtues of models and modelling as an approach to complex urban problems. They will assert, and will be correct in so doing, that much was learned about urban structure and dynamics from these models' efforts. To say the least, there are many and diverse opinions.

It has been suggested that the notion of publishing the results of investigations into pieces of problems was a critical factor in the development of modern science and technology.[1] Further....

A typical scientific paper has never pretended to be more than another little piece in a larger jigsaw – not significant in itself, but as an element in a grander scheme. This technique, of soliciting many modest contributions to the store of human knowledge, has been the secret of Western science since the seventeenth century, for it achieves a corporate, collective power that is far greater than any one individual can exert.[2]

From this point of view, these modelling efforts may be seen in a rather different and more positive light. The model building work reviewed and excerpted here forms the basis for current urban model applications and research.

1. Ziwan, J. M., 'Information, Communication, Knowledge', *Nature* (224) pp. 318–324, 1969.
2. Ziwan, J. M. *op. cit.*

It is true that at its inception, each of the model efforts described here was intended to be complete unto itself. Those model efforts that have failed in this effort did indeed fail. Yet, viewed from a broader perspective, each of these efforts, even the failures, may be considered as contributing to a greater understanding of urban spatial phenomena. Seen from this perspective, urban spatial modelling has come a long way since the early work alluded to in the Swerdloff and Stowers excerpt of chapter 3.

Contemporary practice in urban land use and/or transportation planning makes extensive use of modern computational equipment. Large digital computers are used in many ways. The several functions now served by computer technology fall, roughly, into the following groups:

1. collection, storage, and distribution, including simple descriptive analyses, of enormous quantities of data;
2. complex data analyses including hypothesis testing and theory development;
3. forecasting the consequences and evaluation, of planning alternatives.

A further use sometimes discussed but rarely, if ever, attempted is the actual development and/or design of plans or policies.

The works described in this book fall under headings 2) and 3) above, and pave the way for more reliable and routine type 3) activities along with the continued possibility of eventual work on computerized development and design of plans. At the time of this writing, which is five to ten years after the works described here were completed, we have just come to the point of being competent, at the appropriate levels of spatial and sectoral detail, to make believable forecasts and evaluations of some planning alternatives. This is a heavily qualified statement. Yet, the time frame in which virtually all this work has been done barely spans two decades. And, the work has been chafing at the limits of information processing technology, as well as simple information availability, during the whole of its development. Some of today's routine computational tasks would not have been economically feasible on the computing machinery of fifteen years ago.

Transportation planning *per se* has made effective use of large scale network simulation packages all during the period in which the residential models described here were being developed. Transportation planners seem to have been much more willing to accept the use of the network simulation models than land use planners have been to accept the use of land use simulation models. There are conflicting opinions as to the reasons for this, with some suggestion that transportation planners frequently have more engineering (and thus quantitative) training than land use planners.

It has also been suggested that land use models do not have anything like the reliability of transportation models. The early versions of the transportation models were really no better than the early land use models described here. Without going to lengthy speculation as to differences in training and predisposition towards technological innovations, it may have been that on the surface, the transportation network problems seemed more straightforward. Whatever the other reasons, they were augmented by the fact that the land use model failures always seemed more obvious than those of the transportation models.

All this not withstanding, some of these land use models performed reasonably well. It was no small accomplishment, for example, that the Lowry model population allocations in Pittsburgh, Pa. had R^2 in excess of 0.7 with the observed population distributions. Many of these early models were quite capable of simulating the general spatial patterns of their respective metropolitan areas. They could have been used then to explore metropolitan-wide consequences of many policy alternatives.

Unfortunately, many planners and decision-makers, rather than taking advantage of the models' capabilities (admittedly less than what had first been promised), used their failure to perform well at the individual small zone level as a justification for rejecting the technique entirely. Thus, the years encompassing the model development work described in this book ended with good beginnings towards understanding urban spatial phenomena, but many failures to meet the initial promises made for computer simulation of urban form. Some of the individuals and organizations initially involved moved to other areas of endeavor and, to all intents and purposes, model building activity in the U.S. entered a quiescent period, beginning in the late 1960's and continuing into the mid-1970's.

Just at this time a considerable interest in urban models surfaced in Britain. This interest resulted in work, based on the earlier efforts presented here, which ultimately led to the current state of the modelling art.

5.2. THE CURRENT STATE OF AFFAIRS IN MODELLING

In addition to what has been discussed above, the various reasons for agencies deciding to use or not use models for policy analyses have been very capably discussed elsewhere.[3] Underlying these reasons, at least in

3. Pack, J., 'The Use of Urban Models: Report on a Survey of Planning Organizations', *Journal of the American Institute of Planners*, May 1975.

part, is an inescapable fact. For certain types of analyses, particularly in matters of metropolitan or regional importance, there is no other method which is a sensible alternative to computer simulation models.

The transition from the early residential model efforts described in the materials included in this book to the contemporary models such as the Lowry-Wilson derivatives has been briefly mentioned in chapter 3, section 3.2. As mentioned there, much more detailed descriptions of this newer work may be found in the texts by Wilson and Batty. The question here is one of what the current models can do as far as analysis of planning problems. At present, conventional transportation network models (e.g. the latest FHWA or UMTA packages) and conventional land use models (e.g. the more sophisticated Lowry-Wilson derivatives) are capable of describing 70 percent to 90 percent of the variation in network flows and/or regional activity distributions, respectively. This statement of model capabilities is obviously contingent on several assumptions including stability of parameters and trends as well as of underlying causal structures.

An additional important set of assumptions has to do with levels of areal and sectoral detail. First, it is a fact that with the advent of urban and regional computer simulation models it has become relatively easy to generate prodigious volumes of numerical estimates of all sorts of things. All too often people have been carried away by this capability, and have sometimes confused the mere generation of these numbers with attempts at an accurate replication of reality. The tendency to attempt projections or forecasts at too fine a level of detail remains all too common in computer augmented analyses. Along this line, it remains very unlikely that any computer model, which could be expected to be operational in the foreseeable future, will be capable of producing reliable forecasts at the census tract or any finer level of detail. At a zone size of, say three to five census tracts per zone, and progressing towards further aggregation, one finds a level of detail where it becomes very much more likely that computer model forecasts will be usefully accurate. Finally, as the level of aggregation goes beyond say thirty zones or less in a metropolitan area, the size of the analysis becomes so large that much of the theory on which the models are based becomes obscured and the forecasts are again likely to be unreliable.

To give some specific examples here, the nine county (eight hundred census tract) area around San Francisco, California, seems to be at or slightly beyond the proper limits of disaggregation when considered at the three hundred zone levels. With this same region aggregated to the thirty zone level certain phenomena seem to be well described but others become obscured. An example at a different scale is the Hazleton, Pennsylvania area, population about sixty thousand, in contrast to San Francisco's four and three quarter million, which was modelled reasonably successfully at a one hundred zone level but which probably would have been more appropriately considered at fifty to seventy zones. The determination of an appropriate level of areal detail has a very considerable impact on the determination of the appropriateness of various possible policy analyses. Work done during the DRAM (a recently developed Lowry-PLUM derivative model) calibrations confirmed this hypothesis when, for the same region, the shape (i.e. the parameters) of the best fit distance function changed as the size of the zone at which the analyses were done changed.[4]

Another dimension of level of detail, is sectoral, both in terms of employment classifications as well as population descriptions. Employment classifications have been attempted in urban models at the three and four digit S.I.C. level (yielding hundreds of employment types) at one extreme and at the basic versus non-basic dichotomy at the other extreme. Again, it is difficult to make a precise pronouncement, but something on the order of four to ten employment sectors seems to be an appropriate level of detail. Population too, has been disaggregated to the extreme in some models and considered without any disaggregation in others. Here, the most appropriate level of disaggregation is on the order of four to eight population groups probably based on some combination of income, race, and occupation class.

Finally there is a question as to the appropriate level of aggregation of the transportation network. While here too it is difficult to suggest an arbitrarily exact number of nodes and links, experience suggests that somewhere on the order of eight to twelve times as many network links as there are zones in the areal system would often be an appropriate level of detail.

In the early days of modelling it was often assumed that macro-level trends, being the sum of many micro-level actions, could readily be forecast by summing the results of micro-level models. There still remains today a substantial gap between micro-models of human behavior and macro-models of urban and regional development. The situation in urban modelling today is very like the situation of physics in the late nineteenth century. Newton's theory of mechanics, which worked rather well in many cases was found, at very fine levels of detail and/or in unusual circumstances,

4. Putman, S. H., 'Calibration of Disaggregated Residential Allocation Model – DRAM', *London Papers in Regional Science*, vol. 7, pp. 108–124, 1977.

not to hold true. It took many more years of data collection and observation, along with more than a little flash of genius to produce Einstein's general theory of relativity. It is this author's opinion that while there may, one day, be developed a comprehensive theory tying the micro- and macro-levels together, it is probably not a good idea to simply stop work and wait for such a theory to appear. In the meantime, very good use can be made of the existing macro-models for policy analysis.

Within the approximate limits as to levels of detail mentioned above, there are a wide variety of policy investigations which can readily be handled by computer simulation models. On the occasion that a more detailed level of analysis is desired, the most reasonable approach would be to use computer models to provide inputs to the work of a planner or analyst who is familiar with the geographic area being analyzed. The implication here is that analysis at a finer level of detail than that described above cannot be properly done by a comprehensive urban or regional simulation model. It can and should more properly be done by a competent planner-analyst, familiar with the specific area, and aided by computer analysis of the somewhat larger zones in which the particular area of interest is found.

Despite its obvious reasonableness this type of regional-local, man-machine, cooperation does not seem to be politically feasible. Frequently regional planning agencies (probably the best place for the application of these models) fear the loss of control over their analyses and projection procedures which might result from such arrangements. Yet there are substantial pressures both from within and without to produce forecasts at levels of areal and sectoral detail which are not likely to be possible from computer models for at least another ten years, if ever. One would think that operating agencies would be especially chary of these problems and that there would be some form of internal agency coordination to at least eliminate conflicting internal demands. Yet this author was recently unsuccessful in trying to keep an agency, which should have learned from prior experience, from attempting to forecast more than ten different variables for each of nearly twelve hundred census tracts in a large metropolitan area. One is staggered by the prospect.

There are two similar forms of the same argument that are often raised against the use of models in agencies. First, it is argued that forecasts derived from simple trend or extrapolation procedures can account for just as much of the variance as forecasts from complex simulations. This is probably a true, or nearly true, statement. Second, it may be argued that planners have gotten along without models, and made forecasts that have often been just as good as model forecasts, for some time. This statement, too has frequently been true.

How then can the expense of a modelling effort be justified? While justification of expense is at least in part a function of agency size and responsibility, there remains a compelling reason to consider the use of these models. The name of this reason is interrelatedness. What these models do, which is not attempted by extrapolation and which cannot be done consistently by intuition, is to try to deal with the interdependent aspects of urban systems. It is perfectly clear that planners not utilizing models, base their decisions largely on portions of the same data as that which is available to the models. It is similarly clear that planners are becoming less and less capable of dealing, unassisted, with the increasing number of interactions which are important components of the urban system.

Even in the more sophisticated of contemporary planning agencies there is a dichotomy of staff and responsibilities which militates against truly comprehensive metropolitan or regional planning. The political problems of such multijurisdictional agencies are bad enough, but the continued separation of land use planning staff from transportation planning staff begins to be inexcusable organizational 'thickheadedness'. In many agencies, as a continuation of practices begun twenty or more years ago, the land use staff is entirely separated from the transportation staff. Typically the transportation staff demands inputs, in the form of highly disaggregated forecasts of socioeconomic variables, from the land use staff. These forecasts are used as input to the transportation network programs to generate vehicular trips, to distribute these trips amongst various origins and destinations, and to assign these trips to the transportation network expected to be in place in the forecast year.

On the other side, the land use group demands that the transportation staff provide them with a description of the transportation network expected to be in place in the forecast year. Based usually on the design specifications of this network the land use staff may use one or another of the available urban land use models to forecast the future location of population and employment. The fact that the redistribution of population and employment will alter, via trips and congestion, the observed characteristics of the transportation network is conveniently allowed to fall into the gap between the two planning staffs.

This ignoring of the transportation-land use feedback has resulted among other things, in a long series of surprises for planners, attendant upon the construction of the many urban expressways of the past three decades. It seemed that not only was there an ever increasing spread of urban sprawl, but that many of the new urban expressways achieved the dubious distinction of having 'filled-up' many years in advance of any of the transportation planner's most extravagant estimates. As it appeared less and less likely that construction of additional roads would solve the problem, a number of studies of the matter were undertaken.

This author was given the opportunity in 1971, under the sponsorship of the Federal Highway Administration (FHWA), to do some research into the problem. There were both substantive and methodological outputs from this work.[5] The salient substantive output was further evidence, based on simulation model runs, that a continued policy of urban expressway construction was, in the long run, self-defeating and socially undesirable. Attempts to deal with the problems of urban sprawl and urban traffic congestion simply by constructing additional transportation facilities would result, almost exclusively, in a worsening of both problems. It appeared to be necessary to integrate transportation planning with land use planning, and land use controls, on a regionwide basis, if any improvements in the general situation were to be forthcoming.

The methodological output of the project was the Integrated Transportation and Land Use Package – ITLUP. This package consisted of a set of modified 'off the shelf' models tied together with information flows and feedbacks never before implemented. The fact that the entire project was largely completed by three people for less than one hundred thousand dollars in about a year and one half is some evidence of the benefits to be derived from pursuing this type of research away from the constraints of an operating agency. ITLUP was prepared as a complete set of programs and documentation and was given very limited distribution to various groups in the U.S. The overall structure of the model package involved a simplified, computationally efficient, transportation network package coupled to a modified form of the IPLUM land use model, along with the necessary flow and feedback linkages.[6]

About the time that this first work of ITLUP was completed in the summer of 1973, work began on a separate project designed to test some of the

5. Putman, S. H. et al., 'The Interrelationships of Transportation Development and Land Development' University of Pennsylvania, Department of City and Regional Planning, 1973, revised and reprinted September 1976.
6. Putman, S. H., 'Preliminary Results From An Integrated Transportation and Land Use Models Package', *Transportation*, vol. 3, pp. 193–224, 1974. Putman, S. H., 'Further Results From An Integrated Transportation and Land Use Model Package (ITLUP)', *Transportation Planning and Technology*, vol. 3, pp. 165–173, 1976.

most widely used land use models on a common data base or bases. The IPLUM and EMPIRIC models were ultimately selected for intensive investigation under a National Science Foundation sponsored project. In the course of this work it was discovered that the procedures for parameter estimation for the Lowry-IPLUM types of model had never been properly developed or applied in U.S. modelling practice. The lead of British researchers in the field was followed in this matter, and a report comparing the two model types was published in the autumn of 1976.[7] Briefly stated, the report concluded that EMPIRIC produced somewhat better fits to base year data than DRAM (the revised Lowry-IPLUM derivative model). This modest advantage was, however, overwhelmed by the inadequate and often inappropriate response of EMPIRIC to variable manipulation and simulated policy inputs.

Based on these results, further work has now been undertaken, under the National Science Foundation and the Urban Mass Transit Administration to make these new models widely available at minimum cost to planning professionals and agencies. One of the arguments against urban simulation models has been the substantial costs of developing these models for the various agencies wishing to use them. Even after a model was developed and made operational, the programs were often so complex as to defy routine usage and thus inevitably led to the models' abandonment as an instrument for policy analyses. Thus present model development work must focus on, in addition to reliability of forecasts, reduction of the costs of implementation, and simplification of procedures for use. These must include not only procedures for the use of the model, but straightforward and well documented procedures for estimating the model's parameters as well. The procedures now being prepared for distribution attempt to overcome these problems. All of this would not have been possible without the work described in this book as a basis on which to build.

5.3. SUMMING UP

When, in the early 1960's, the first urban computer simulation models were being developed, one of the principal goals was to develop the capability of assessing the consequences of various urban renewal plans on the spatial

7. Putman, S. H., 'Laboratory Testing of Predictive Land Use Models: Some Comparisons', Report of Results from National Science Foundation Grant – GI-38978, published by the U.S. Department of Transportation, Office of Transportation Systems Analysis and Information, October 1976.

distribution of activities. Unfortunately, it was to take more than a decade of additional research to get anywhere near having models with such capabilities.

The land use component of an integrated set of land use and transportation models would produce estimates of activity levels in each zone which are sensitive to: (1) the mix of activities in that zone and, to a lesser extent, in adjacent zones; (2) the density and degree of existing development; (3) the availability of land in the zone; and (4) a measure of the spatial separation of the activities from each other. One such model package, ITLUP, will estimate three to five basic employment sectors, two to four non-basic employment sectors, and four types of population. Any policy which can be described as either directly or indirectly altering any of the factors which determine the location of these activities will be testable with the model package.

A number of different public policies could alter the mix of activities in a zone and could enter the models in various forms. The arrival or departure of an employment facility would induce significant effects in the model outputs. The arrival of a number of households of a particular income class might well result in changes in location of other households and perhaps of some employees too. Similarly the departure of a group of households would probably further induce changes in a zone's activity mix.

The density and degree, or extent, of development in a zone could also be affected by policy inputs. Clearance of certain types of structure would change density as would the erection of new structures. The construction of a large new development, say of single family residential homes, or – at a different density – of apartments, would change both the zone's density as well as its extent of development. These changes would induce other changes, both in employment and in population location. In a related way, changes in the amount of land available in a zone will affect future location of activities in a zone. More stringent land use controls, having the effect of reducing available land, will change the pattern of activities locating in a zone. Similarly, holding back land from development will also result in changed location patterns.

Finally, the spatial separation of activities from each other is a key variable in these models. This variable is usually expressed in terms of travel times and/or travel costs between zones and activities. Thus any substantial change in the transportation facilities will result in a change in activity distributions. Even network changes on a particular link, i.e. new construction or increased congestion, will result in changes in a zone's activity distribution. Various public policies will affect the transport system in these ways. The most obvious of these has been the construction of highways which, with their awesome proliferation, have indelibly altered the distributions of activities throughout every part of the nation. Modifications to individual or groups of links in the transport system will induce alterations in the traffic flows as well as changes in the distributions of activities. Similarly, changes in link capacity will induce these same effects by virtue of the link's not becoming as rapidly congested as it did prior to the addition of that new capacity.

Thus, in the late 1970's, we are at the point of having models which can be readily applied to a number (though certainly not all) of policy issues. These techniques are useful now only because of the work which has gone before. Yet today's techniques are not an end to the process of learning, and subsequently applying, more about urban spatial phenomena. Today's techniques are the basis for the next decade's research efforts in this vein.

This book represents an attempt to collect in one place and present in a coherent framework the most interesting and important work in urban residential simulation modelling up to (approximately) 1970. This work is the basis for most of that which has been done since 1970. As such, it represents the initial postulating and testing of hypotheses concerning the observable determinants of urban residential spatial patterns. It is to be hoped that the effort spent on this collection is justified in that it will provide a background for both planners and researchers who are involved (or are likely to become so) in work with contemporary urban simulation.

Studies in applied regional science

Vol. 1
On the use of input-output models for regional planning
W. A. Schaffer

This volume is devoted to the use of input-output techniques in regional planning. The study provides a clear introduction to the essential ideas of input-output analysis. Particular emphasis is placed on the intricate problems of data collection at a regional level.

ISBN 90 207 0626 8

Vol. 2
Forecasting transportation impacts upon land use
P. F. Wendt

This reader concentrates on transportation problems in urban areas. After a survey of model techniques for analyzing transportation and land use problems, several new methods in the field of transportation and land-use planning are presented.

ISBN 90 207 0627 6

Vol. 3
Estimation of stochastic input-output models
S. D. Gerking

The primary objective of this monograph is to develop a method for measuring the uncertainty in estimates of the technical coefficients in an input-output model. This study also describes three further applications of the two-stage least squares estimation technique in an input-output context.

ISBN 90 207 0628 4

Martinus Nijhoff Publishing

Vol. 4
Locational behavior in manufacturing industries
William R. Latham III

Agglomerative economies form a central concept in
regional science. Yet an empirical determination of
agglomeration advantages has been minimal up to now.
To help remedy the situation, this study contains an
effort to gauge the order of magnitude of agglomeration
advantages, based on a careful inspection of industrial
location data.

ISBN 90 207 0638 1

Vol. 5
Regional economic structure and environmental pollution
B.E.M.G. Coupé

This book deals with the ever-increasing problem of
pollution. The author has constructed an extensive
interregional model for economic activities and pollution.
   Coupé's two-region model is used to calculate an
equilibrium in terms of production and pollution abate-
ment.

ISBN 90 207 0646 2

Vol. 6
The demand for urban water
P. Darr, S. L. Feldman, C. Kamen

The range of choice for water management can include
adjustments to remedy disequilibria through
management of the demand side of the market. This
volume explores the components affecting demands
using combined economic, engineering and social
psychological tools and recommends remedies in tariff
design to conform to basic economic postulates.

ISBN 90 207 0647 0

Martinus Nijhoff Publishing

Vol. 7
Production systems and hierarchies of centres
J. Gunnarsson

In this study hierarchies of centres are discussed, with special references to Tinbergen-Bos systems. The author also uses component analysis to examine whether the structure of the Swedish system of centres resembles the structure of different hierarchy models.

Relations between regularities for optimal systems (the size-distribution of centres and space-functional relations between types of centres) and input-output coefficients as well as the location of natural resources are studied, and a quadratic programming model is proposed. This extension of the problem makes it possible to determine capacities of plants and systems of centres simultaneously. Thus, distribution of plant sizes and city sizes may be studied in the same model.

ISBN 90 207 0688 8

Vol. 8
Multi-criteria analysis and regional decision-making
A. van Delft and P. Nijkamp

The study focuses on the use of multi-criteria methods as a tool for adequate decision-making. After a discussion of traditional evaluation techniques (cost-benefit analysis, for instance) several multi-criteria decision methods are reviewed. Particular attention is paid to 'concordance analysis' as it is called. Several variants of this new evaluation method are developed. The operational aspects of concordance analysis are highlighted particularly in the case of conflicting views on regional growth and environmental protection.

ISBN 90 207 0689 6

Martinus Nijhoff Publishing

Vol. 9
Economic aspects of regional welfare
C. P. A. Bartels

This study is focused on the analysis of relationships
between various economic aspects of regional welfare,
especially income distribution and unemployment. A
wide variety of methodological questions are explored,
with a particular emphasis on their empirical relevance.

Methods for describing income distributions concisely
and exploring characteristics of regional unemployment
series and alternative ways of defining income inequality
measures are considered, with a special emphasis on a full
explicit integration of normative and positive elements in
this definition. Characteristics of unemployment series are
also empirically explored. A link is made between income
and employment based on an explanatory analysis, and the
study concludes with the presentation of a scheme for an
integrated regional labour market/income distribution model.

ISBN 90 207 0706 X

Vol. 10
Spatial representation and spatial interaction
Ian Masser and P. J. B. Brown

This book is directed towards regional scientists, geo-
graphers, urban, regional and transport planners and others
with a particular interest in the practical application of
methods of spatial analysis. In recent years, the problem of
spatial representation has been recognized as being of
fundamental importance to the effective application of a

Martinus Nijhoff Publishing

wide range of analytical methods. This book draws together for the first time various related pieces of work undertaken in the field of spatial interaction research and sets them in a general framework within which the problem of spatial representation is viewed as part of the general problem of aggregation. Two kinds of strategy for dealing with this problem in relation to interaction data are outlined in an introductory overview of the field and their practical application is illustrated in subsequent chapters. In the concluding chapter, a number of general themes from the various streams of work are identified and a number of areas defined for further investigation.

ISBN 90 207 0717.5

Vol. 11
Tourism and regional growth
Moheb Ghali, editor

This book is the first systematic empirical study of the growth operations open to a region, the tourist-oriented economy of Hawaii.

The first part is devoted to studying regional growth under resource constraints. This is followed by the study of the region's major exports, their determinants, and projections of their future growth. An econometric model of regional growth is presented in the third part and is utilized to simulate the growth paths of income, employment, migration and unemployment under alternative tourism policies. In the last part of the book, the fiscal implications of the alternative growth paths are derived.

ISBN 90 207 0716 7

Martinus Nijhoff Publishing

Vol. 12
Economies of scale in manufacturing location
Gerald A. Carlino

While agglomeration economies have been of paramount importance in explaining the relative concentration of manufacturing activity in metropolitan or central places, they have not been adequately measured or tested. Most attempts at measuring agglomeration economies have been indirect rather than direct. e.g., Marcus' residual growth proxy or Edel's elasticity of land values with respect to city size measurement. The present volume suggests a more direct method of quantifying this rather elusive variable, through the application of production function techniques. Also, questions concerning optimal city size and industrial location are considered.

ISBN 90 207 0721 3

m)